Spell it out

Also by David Crystal

The Cambridge encyclopedia of language

The Cambridge encyclopedia of the English language

The stories of English

The fight for English

Think on my words: an introduction to Shakespeare's language

Txting: the gr8 db8

By hook or by crook: a journey in search of English

A little book of language

Evolving English: one language, many voices

Begat: the King James Bible and the English language

Internet linguistics

Just a phrase I'm going through: my life in language

The story of English in 100 words

Spell It Out

The Curious, Enthralling, and
Extraordinary Story of English Spelling

David Crystal

St. Martin's Press ✹ New York

SPELL IT OUT. Copyright © 2012 by David Crystal. All rights reserved.
Printed in the United States of America. For information, address
St. Martin's Press, 175 Fifth Avenue, New York, N.Y. 10010.

www.stmartins.com

ISBN 978-1-250-00347-8 (hardcover)
ISBN 978-1-250-02886-0 (e-book)

St. Martin's Press books may be purchased for educational, business,
or promotional use. For information on bulk purchases, please contact
Macmillan Corporate and Premium Sales Department at 1-800-221-
7945 extension 5442 or write specialmarkets@macmillan.com.

First published in Great Britain by Profile Books Ltd

First U.S. Edition: June 2013

10 9 8 7 6 5 4 3 2 1

Contents

Introduction

I have wanted to write a book on English spelling all my life, but the prospect has always scared me. There is simply so much of it. With well over a million words in English, affected in myriad ways by some 1,300 years of history, the task of attempting to find some order in the chaos, as linguists like to do, seemed well nigh impossible. In 2005 I compiled a *Pocket Spelling Dictionary* for Penguin Books, and that reinforced my feeling about the vast scale of any such enterprise.

What has changed is that sophisticated tools to help carry out this task have now become available. Chief among these is the online *Oxford English Dictionary*, which makes it possible to see the spelling history of any word at the click of a mouse. And two huge item-by-item surveys have taken place – the first by Edward Carney, published in 1994 as *A Survey of English Spelling*; the second by Christopher Upward, published in 2011 in association with George Davidson as *A History of English Spelling*. It was my privilege to edit the latter book as part of the Blackwell/Wiley Language Library, and it was in the course of this exercise that I began to realise that most of the required hard linguistic graft – the collection and arrangement of copious examples, letter by letter, period by period – had been done.

Bridges now need to be built between this solid academic linguistic foundation and the curiosity of the general English-using public, whose common cry in this connection is 'Why on earth is — spelled like that?' A huge number of words can fill that blank, and this book deals with quite a few of them. The bridges are especially needed by teachers, who have the unenviable task of introducing their students to the English orthographic world. The student constituency is twofold: children learning to read and write English as a mother-tongue; and the vast number of children and adults who are learning English as a foreign language. The complaint from all of them resounds around the globe: can anything be done to facilitate the task of learning to spell English words? I believe the answer is yes, though a new pedagogy will take a while to implement. The present unsatisfactory teaching situation is the result of several centuries of evolution, and it will take some time to replace this by a more efficient approach based on sound linguistic principles. I make some suggestions about such an approach in the final two chapters of the book.

Nowhere is the old saying 'I can't see the wood for the trees' more applicable than in the case of spelling. We are dealing with thousands of words whose orthographic character has been shaped by sets of factors that often defy generalisation. We search for rules, and just when we think we have found some, we encounter a host of anomalies, variations and exceptions. How, under these circumstances, do we find a road map to take us through the spelling wood?

I believe the best way into the wood is chronological. To understand the complexity of English spelling, we first have to understand when and how the language was originally written down. So our story begins with the Anglo-Saxon monks, using our knowledge of Modern English to give us a sense of the scale of the task they faced (Chapters 2–3). The system they devised was a good one, but it had weaknesses, and these are the source of many modern spelling difficulties (Chapters 4–7). The arrival of the French in 1066 brought a new set of attitudes and practices: a French approach to spelling was grafted onto the Anglo-Saxon system. This, along with the changes that were taking place in the spoken English of the time, brought a radical transformation in English spelling (Chapters 8–15).

The Middle English period, from the 12th to the 15th centuries, is hugely different from its Old English predecessor. Thousands of words entered the English language, especially from French and Latin, and they all had to be spelled. Words began to influence each other in unexpected ways (Chapters 16 and 17). A fundamental change in English pronunciation had to be handled (Chapter 18). And the introduction of printing introduced a new perspective which had both strengths and weaknesses (Chapter 19). By the 16th century, the demand had grown for spelling reform, but this proved difficult to implement (Chapter 20). Writers turned increasingly to the history of words (etymology) as a means of regularising spelling, and although this perspective brought its own complications, an etymological approach does explain a great deal of the irregularity seen in Modern English (Chapters 21–3).

Since the 17th century, people have searched for other ways of coping with the vagaries of English spelling. Some have put their faith in rules (Chapter 24); some in dictionaries (Chapters 25–6); some in publishers' house styles and printers' manuals (Chapter 27). But the huge growth of English vocabulary, fuelled especially by the global spread of the language and the arrival of the Internet, has greatly increased the amount of orthographic diversity (Chapters 28–9). Commercial, literary and domestic settings have used spelling variation as a means of expressing their identity (Chapter 30). Further dimensions to the character of English orthography are seen in the idiosyncratic spellings of personal names and place names (Chapter 31), the continuing growth in exotic loanwords (Chapter 32–3), the spelling of interjections (Chapter 34), and the use of abbreviations and symbols (Chapter 35). Only a linguistic perspective, I conclude in Chapters 36 and 37, can bring some degree of order into the resulting chaos, as we look towards the future. And for teachers, I argue in two appendices, this perspective is essential.

1

The nature of the problem

English spelling is difficult, but it is not as chaotic as is often claimed. An explanatory perspective can make the learning of spelling easier.

Why is English spelling so difficult? Why do we have spelling bees and competitions? Why do children spend so much time learning lists of spellings off by heart? Why do so many people feel they are bad at spelling, and worry so much about it? And why are good spellers so proud of their achievement that, when they see a misspelling, they condemn the writer as sloppy, careless, lazy or uneducated?

Spelling is evidently important. Society says so. When people notice spelling mistakes in a newspaper or poster, they react – with emotions ranging from mild amusement to horrified disgust. Publishers employ proofreaders to prevent such things happening. Some employers have told me that if they see a job application with spelling mistakes, it goes into the bin straight away. We are under similar pressures online: to access an Internet address, we have to get the spelling exactly right.

Society expects us to spell perfectly. And yet we are all aware that there are some words in the language that we don't know how to spell, and have to look them up before we write them. There are no exceptions. Nobody knows how to spell every word in the language. Even the brilliant spellers who win the prizes in spelling bees get some words wrong.

People provide aids to help us achieve that perfection: dictionaries and spelling checkers. But there are problems with both. To look a word up in a dictionary, we have to know how to spell it – which rather defeats the purpose of the exercise. We'll find it eventually, of course, but it isn't the most obvious way to deal with the difficulty. And spelling checkers are useful only to a limited extent. They spot spellings that don't exist; but they won't highlight a word if it's misspelled yet does exist. The first two stanzas of an ode to a spelling checker, by Mark Eckman and Jerrold H. Zar, illustrate the problem:

I have a spelling checker,
It came with my PC.
It plane lee marks four my revue
Miss steaks aye can knot sea.

Eye ran this poem threw it,
Your sure reel glad two no.
Its vary polished in it's weigh.
My checker tolled me sew.

A spelling checker wouldn't spot anything wrong here.

One day spelling checkers will be more sophisticated, taking the context of the word into account; but for now they can let us down badly. One day there'll be even better labour-saving spelling devices. We will speak into a machine and it will spell the words out for us, or type them for us. Devices of this kind already exist, using voice-to-text software, but they're far from perfect. They don't like broad regional accents. They don't like fast speakers. They don't like background noise. They especially don't like proper names. Eventually these problems will be solved – but not for another generation or so.

So in the short term we need to spell as best we can – and maybe even in the long term. After all, none of these devices will work at all if our computer or phone runs out of power. And if we want to write when we've no electronic equipment to hand, the responsibility remains with us.

What can we do to make the task of learning to spell easier? My answer is in a word: EXPLAIN it. I believe the first step in solving a problem is to see why the problem exists. If we understand why English spelling is apparently in such a mess, we remove part of the barrier. Explaining why words are spelled the way they are can help us remember them. The stories behind the spellings are often fascinating, and interest adds motivation. I've told some of them to young schoolchildren, and their comments warm my linguistic heart. 'I'll never forget there's an *h* in *ghost* now,' said one to me, with a big smile on her face. Yes!

Note I say 'apparently in such a mess'. English spelling isn't as bad as most people think it is. They describe it as 'chaotic', 'inconsistent', 'irregular', 'unpredictable', 'unlearnable'. Thomas Sheridan, the 18th-century elocutionist, went so far as to say that the state of our spelling system is worse than 'the darkest hieroglyphics or most difficult ciphers which the art of man has hitherto invented'. The impression is fuelled by writers who have gone out of their way to draw attention to the irregularities.

A famous example dates from the middle of the 19th century, and came to be associated in the 20th century with George Bernard Shaw: *ghoti* is said to spell *fish*, because *f* is spelled *gh* as in *cough*, *i* is spelled *o* as in *women*, and *sh* is spelled *ti* as in *nation*. This is complete naughtiness. The spelling *ti* is NEVER used with this sound at the end of a word in English, and the spelling *gh* is NEVER used with this sound at the beginning of a word. But people have been taken in by this sort of nonsense. And the feeling that English spelling is a mess has been reinforced by the clever creations based on irregular forms, such as 'Though the rough cough and hiccough plough me through, I ought to cross the lough.' All good fun, but hugely misleading as a summary of the English spelling system. It's a bit like listing eight accident blackspots in a country, and saying all the roads are like that.

English spelling isn't as chaotic as Shaw suggests. It isn't 'unlearnable'. You, reader, have learned to decode it, otherwise you wouldn't even be reading this. And there are thousands of English words that you have no trouble spelling at all. So how did you manage it? You probably have a vague memory of spelling tests and lists, but how did you actually get from that stage of early learning to your present level of competence? Somehow, over several years, you worked out the system and took on board the exceptions. You have quite a powerful 'spelling engine' in your head, which enables you to see a new word and make a reasonable shot at how to pronounce it (text to speech) and hear a new word and make a reasonable guess about how to write it down (speech to text).

But not all words are easy to say and write. And it takes several years to get to the stage where our spelling engine purrs along nicely. So anything we can do to make learning to spell easier – both for children learning their mother-tongue and foreigners learning English as a foreign language – must be a good thing. Some people think spelling reform is the best way forward. But whether we believe in spelling reform or not, the first step is to understand the present English spelling system. And that's what this book aims to do. It explains why English spelling has come to be the way it is. It isn't the whole solution. We still have to work at it, to become a good speller. But it's half the battle.

And we begin, as all good explanations must, at the beginning.

Pooh and his friends on spelling

Pooh said to Piglet: 'It's all right, Piglet. Spelling is easy once you get started.'
Piglet nodded. 'Getting started is the worst bit.'
…
Christopher Robin jumped onto the tree stump and made an announce-
ment. 'Friends, the Spelling Bee has been cancelled, because spelling is difficult enough at the best of times, and impossible in the rain.'

(David Benedictus, *Return to the Hundred Acre Wood*, 2009, Ch. 2, 'In which Owl does
a crossword, and a Spelling Bee is held')

You can't help respecting anybody who can spell TUESDAY, even if he
doesn't spell it right; but spelling isn't everything. There are days when spelling Tuesday simply doesn't count.

(Rabbit of Owl, in A. A. Milne, *The House at Pooh Corner*, 1928, Ch. 5)

2

The beginning

The origins of the English writing system lie in the alphabet the Romans used for Latin. The task of adaptation was a priority for the monks in Anglo-Saxon England.

Imagine. You are one of the missionaries arriving in Britain in the 6th century AD. You discover a place largely ruled by Anglo-Saxons, in several kingdoms, speaking dialects of a Germanic language brought from the Continent a century before. Your job is to introduce Christianity into the country. Charters have to be agreed with kings. Letters sent out. Churches established. Local organisers have to be trained. Priests need to compose prayers and homilies in Anglo-Saxon so that ordinary people will understand them. A priority, in short, is to get the language written down.

You look around, and you see a few signs of writing already there. Some are memories of the days when the Romans ruled, centuries before. Inscriptions on old walls, buildings and monuments. A few coins and objects with writing on them. But they are all Latin words and names, not Anglo-Saxon ones. No help there.

You find that some of the Anglo-Saxons do know how to write. The early settlers had brought a runic alphabet with them from Europe, and used the letters to write names or charms on swords, brooches, rings and other objects, as well as on gravestones and buildings. The rune-carvers, or rune-masters, were special people. Runes were mysterious and magical. The very word 'rune' means 'something hidden' or 'secret'. Why not use those? Unfortunately, you can't. As a Christian monk, you have a problem. Runes are too strongly associated with magic, dark forces and the pagan practices you want to eradicate.

The Roman alphabet, on the other hand, has all the right associations for you and your colleagues. It has been used for centuries as a medium of Christian expression. You've been reading St Jerome's Latin Bible as long as you can remember. Several beautiful handwritten forms of Roman letters exist, especially in Ireland. You and all your colleagues know that alphabet well. It's the obvious choice. All you have to do is write down the sounds of Anglo-Saxon using the Roman letters. You have twenty-three at your disposal: A B C D E F G H I K L M N O P Q R S T V X Y Z. That should be more than enough, you think.

You quickly realise that you're wrong. You listen carefully to Anglo-Saxon – or English, as it would later be called – and you hear sounds that don't exist in Latin. Two sounds especially catch your attention: consonant sounds made by the tongue between the teeth (we'd call them 'th' sounds today, as in *this* and *thin*). How are you going to write those? There also seem to be far more sounds in this language than in Latin. What on earth are you going to do?

The abbot calls a meeting in the scriptorium, where all manuscript work takes place. 'We are going to have to adapt the Roman alphabet [he says in Latin] to make it work. Any suggestions?'

3

The size of the problem

The origins of spelling difficulties in English lie in the fact that there are far more sounds in the language than there are letters, as can be seen from a list of the spoken vowels and consonants that have to be written down. Phonetic symbols help to explain problem cases in later chapters.

Old English, the language spoken by the Anglo-Saxons in Britain, is dead and gone. We speak and write Modern English now. But we can get a sense of the scale of the problem facing the monks if we transfer their task to the present day. If we had to write down Modern English in Britain with a different letter for every distinctive sound, just how many letters would we need?

The first thing we have to do is establish how many distinctive sounds there are. We do this by finding all the words that change their meaning when just one of their sounds is altered. We might start with *pip*, and change the first sound. *Tip* is different from *pip*. So is *sip*, and *hip*, and *lip*… That gives us a *p, t, s, h, l* … Then we could change the second sound. *Pip* is different from *pop* and *pup* and *peep* …

That gives us *i, o, u, ee* ... Linguists call these distinctive sounds 'phonemes'. How many phonemes are there in English? The answer depends on the regional accent we have, but for many people the total is forty-four. That's the number we hear, for example, in the British accent known as 'Received Pronunciation' (RP), widely understood in the UK because it's used by many presenters on national radio and television. The corresponding accent in the USA is known as General American.

To understand how English spelling works, it's essential to develop a sense of what sounds have to be written down. So I list below all the phonemes in these two accents, using the system presented by John Wells in his classic study, *Accents of English*. Don't pay attention to the spellings at this point. Simply say the words aloud and listen to the sounds that the spellings convey to you. Phoneticians have given each phoneme its own symbol to show that it's different from the others. And to show that we're talking about sounds, not letters, these symbols are put in slant brackets.

It's not important, at this point in the book, to remember all the symbols. But do keep a bookmark on this page, because in order to explain certain spellings I will sometimes have to show the pronunciation of the words, especially in the older period of the language, and that is where you will see these symbols used. For the present, it's important only to appreciate the number of phonemes there are in English.

There are twenty-four consonant phonemes in both Received Pronunciation and General American.

/p/ as in pin, apple, rip
/b/ as in big, table, rob
/t/ as in top, writer, pot
/d/ as in dog, radar, bed
/k/ as in kin, taking, rock
/g/ as in got, bigger, hug
/f/ as in fat, rifle, off
/v/ as in van, saving, love
/θ/ as in thin, earthly, path
/ð/ as in this, mother, seethe
/s/ as in sit, rustic, pass
/z/ as in zip, buzzer, has
/ʃ/ as in shop, bishop, mash
/ʒ/ as in gigolo, confusion, mirage
/tʃ/ as in chest, butcher, catch
/dʒ/ as in jest, badger, lodge
/h/ as in hot, unhand
/m/ as in map, summer, dim
/n/ as in net, deny, win
/ŋ/ as in hanger, sing
/l/ as in lip, police, fool
/r/ as in rip, carrot, and in General American also
     after a vowel, as in star
/w/ as in well, unwilling
/j/ as in you, beyond

There are up to twenty vowel phonemes in these accents, and the way they are used varies a little between British and American English, though not enough to cause any real problems of intelligibility.

We understand each other well enough.

When you see a colon (:) after a symbol, it means that the sound is long, with a single phonetic quality throughout. If there is no colon, the vowel sound is short. When you see a combination of two symbols, it means that the sound is long because it has two distinct phonetic qualities; such sounds are called 'diphthongs', and they play a particularly important role in the history of English spelling.

/ɪ/ as in kit, sister, filling

/e/ as in met, dress, spelling

/æ/ as in cat, trap, magnify

/ɒ/ as in lot, got, cloth, gone; in General American,
    /ɑ/ as in lot, gotten, /ɔ/ as in cloth, gone

/ʌ/ as in cup, strut, buckle

/ʊ/ as in foot, look, put

/ə/ as in the, sof<u>a</u>, pr<u>o</u>fess

/i:/ as in see, fleece, eating

/ɑ:/ as in bath, palm, start; in General American,
    /æ/ as in bath, /ɑ/ as in palm, /ɑr/ as in start

/u:/ as in soon, goose, tube

/ɔ:/ as in thought, north, force; in General
    American, /ɔ/ as in thought, /ɔr/ as in north,
    /or/ as in force

/ɜ:/ as in nurse, bird, sermon; in General
    American, /ɜr/ as in nurse, bird, sermon

/eɪ/ as in aim, face, delay

/aɪ/ as in I, price, deny

/ɔɪ/ as in oil, choice, boy

/əʊ/ as in oh, goat, below

/aʊ/ as in owl, mouth, cow

/ɪə/ as in ear, beard, near; in General American,
   /ɪr/ as in ear, beard, near
/ɛə/ as in air, fairy, square; in General American,
   /ɛr/ as in air, fairy, square
/ʊə/ as in cure, your, fury; in General American,
   /ʊr/ as in cure, your, fury

Of course, if you don't speak with either a Received Pronunciation or a General American accent, you may find you have a different number of phonemes. The traditional Cockney accent of London, for example, doesn't use the two 'th' sounds; they use /f/ and /v/ instead. For a Cockney, *fin* and *thin* sound the same; so do *vat* and *that*. But whichever accent you have – Canadian, Australian, Irish, Indian, Nigerian ... – you'll be using a similar number: forty or so.

To write them all down in a completely regular way, we would need an alphabet of the same size. And that is what we haven't got. We have an alphabet of only twenty-six letters. How are we going to spell forty+ phonemes with twenty-six letters? That, in a nutshell, is the problem of English spelling.

4
Building the alphabet

Adapting the Latin alphabet to English meant the addition of extra letters. The result was a phonetic system in which every letter was sounded.

The problem was the same in Anglo-Saxon times. The Christian missionaries had an alphabet of twenty-three Roman letters to spell a language that, at the time, had at least thirty-seven phonemes (scholars argue about the exact number). So one of the first things they must have done was look for some extra letters. In particular, how were they going to solve the problem of those 'th' sounds? These were really noticeable, as they were used in some very common words, such as *this* and *thing*, as well as in the names of men and women, such as *Cuthbert* and *Ethel*.

Today, we'd solve the problem by setting up a national committee, or maybe a social networking site, and get a discussion going. In the 600s, monks would have been thinking about the question in monasteries at opposite ends of the country – Canterbury, Winchester, Glastonbury, Jarrow – with no chance of regular joint consultation. There was an urgency to provide written material in English. So it isn't surprising to find that different monastic communities arrived at different solutions.

There are, after all, several possible ways of solving the 'th' problem. A scribe could create a new letter from scratch. He could find a 'th' letter from some other writing system. He could use an existing letter in a new way – perhaps spelling the sound as 'tt'. He could use two (or more) different letters to spell it – 'th' or 'dh', for instance. He could join two letters together, much as we sometimes see in Modern English *encyclopædia*. Or he could add an extra mark to a letter (a diacritic, or accent mark), such as we see today in *é* or *ñ*.

The earliest manuscripts show that different writers made different choices. Some scribes, especially in the north of England, went for the two-letter solution, using *th*. Some simply used a *d*. But before long most seem to have gone down the 'new letter' route. Or rather, routes. For *two* new letters came to be used for 'th'. One seems to have come from the alphabet already devised for writing Irish. This was a 'd' with a thin line through a slanting ascender. In modern typography it's usually shown as 'ð' – and phoneticians use it for one of the 'th' sounds, as seen in Chapter 3. Its name in Old English was ð*æt* ('that'), but in the 19th century it came to be called 'eth'.

The other new letter was borrowed from the runic alphabet: a rune called 'thorn', perhaps because of its shape – 'þ'. Whoever first suggested it can't have been too bothered by the pagan associations of runes. Perhaps by the 7th century the magical associations were no longer being viewed as an issue. Or perhaps the idea was to 'exorcise' them by using runic symbols in a Christian context.

Eth and thorn both came to be widely used, and quickly replaced the early spellings of *th* and *d*. They are one of the most distinctive features of Anglo-Saxon writing. By the 8th century, they seem to be used interchangeably. The same word is spelled with thorn in one manuscript and with eth in another – *þing* and *ðing* for 'thing', for example – and sometimes both spellings occur in the *same* manuscript. There are so few surviving Anglo-Saxon manuscripts from the early period that it's difficult to know what factors governed the choice. Perhaps the two letters reflected a scribe's attempt to show they had different sounds in his accent (as with the phonetic distinction shown in Chapter 3). Perhaps the choice of letter was a matter of personal taste – a writer liking the look of one more than the other. Perhaps it was the fashion to use just one of the letters in a scriptorium. Perhaps a scribe found one of the letters easier to write. Perhaps he liked variation for its own sake (there being no notion of 'correct' spelling in those days). Or perhaps he didn't even notice that he was varying the spelling, any more than today people don't notice they write an 's' in different ways in informal 'joined-up' (cursive) writing. Whatever the reasons, there was a huge amount of variation, and usage changed over time. Up to around the reign of King Alfred, in the 9th century, eth was the dominant form; then thorn came to be increasingly used, especially at the beginnings of words.

The monks also seem to have had a problem over how to write down the sound of /w/, as in *we*. This sound had once been used in Latin, spelled with a V, but by the 7th century this letter was being pronounced with a /v/ sound. That didn't seem to bother some scribes, especially in the north of England, who began spelling the English /w/ with a *u* – the form of V used as a small letter in cursive writing. Others must have found this to be confusing, because they opted for a *uu* ('double u') instead. But most scribes, especially in the south of England, can't have been convinced by either of these choices, because we soon find them going down a different path – using a new letter, taken (once again) from the runic alphabet. They chose the rune named 'wyn', meaning 'joy'– ᚹ – and this became the commonest usage throughout the Anglo-Saxon period. (It died out in the 13th century, when the 'double u', now joined together as a single letter *w*, became the norm.)

The monks must also have puzzled over the sound of the vowel they heard in such words as *man* and *at*. It wasn't quite like the Latin sound spelled with an *a*, which was lower and further back in the mouth. In fact, it sounded almost like the /e/ of a word like *set*. A sound halfway between *a* and *e*? Why not write it with both letters, then? And this is what we find, in the early manuscripts: *ae*. By the end of the 8th century, scribes had joined the letters together as *æ*. Modern scholars, needing a name for this new letter, and trying to capture the spirit of the time, looked to the runic alphabet, where the /a/ sound was represented by a rune called 'ash'. So they called it that.

At that point, the monks must have felt that these four additions were all they needed, because they stayed with this alphabet of twenty-seven letters:

a, æ, b, c, d, e, f, g, h, i, k, l, m, n, o, p, q, r, s, t, þ, ð, u, ρ, x, y, z

However, they made very little use of four of them. Early manuscripts show occasional instances of *q* (followed by *u*), but these were soon replaced by *cw*. There are hardly any instances of *k* and *z*. And *x* appears in just a few words, such as *axe* and *oxa* ('ox'). The main difference between Old and Modern English alphabets is the absence of *j* and *v*, which didn't arrive until the Middle Ages, as we shall see.

Several of the Anglo-Saxon letters were written in unfamiliar ways, to modern eyes, showing the influence of the Irish way of writing known to the early missionaries. The letter *s*, for example, was usually elongated, rather like ʃ. And the letter *g* was written with a distinctive ȝ shape, which, centuries later, in the Middle English period, needed its own name, and came to be called 'yogh'. This is an important point, as it explains some later developments in spelling. More on it in due course.

Although well short of the total number of phonemes in Old English, this alphabet was plainly enough for the monks to write down what they were hearing. And that's what they did. The evidence is in the variant spellings which reflect the pronunciation of different dialects. Remember that there was no notion of 'correct' or 'standard' spelling at the outset. So, if people in the north of England said the word for 'land' with rounded lips, so that it sounded like 'lond', then it would be spelled that way, with an *o*. A much more standard form of spelling did eventually emerge, but not until the later part of the Old English period.

On the whole, the monks did a good job when they wrote English down for the first time. Adapting the Latin alphabet to English worked well enough. And they thought in a phonetic way. Every letter was pronounced: there were no 'silent' letters. The word for 'know' was spelled *cnawan*, and that initial *c* was sounded. So was the *w* of *writan* (silent today in *write*), the *g* of *gnæt* (silent today in *gnat*), and many more. It sounds like an ideal system. But the monks weren't linguists, and their system had weaknesses. Some were serious, and would keep spelling enthusiasts and reformers preoccupied for the next thousand years. *Coughs* and *hiccoughs*? The problem starts here.

Letter origins

A, a

A has been the first letter of the alphabet for the whole of its history. Originally a consonant, *aleph* (meaning 'ox'), in the Semitic alphabet, it became the vowel *alpha* in Greek. The lower-case 'open a' is a development of the capital letter, with the addition of a left-facing loop at the top and a lowering of the cross-bar. The lower-case 'closed *a*' is an italic development from the medieval period.

B, b

B has been the second letter of the alphabet since Semitic times, a consonant whose name was *beth* (meaning 'house'). It emerged in the later Greek alphabet as a capital letter with a shape close to its modern form. The lower-case letter developed from a later style of handwriting consisting of simple rounded letter shapes.

C, c

C has been the third letter of the alphabet since Semitic times, developing its right-facing curve in the Latin alphabet. The lower-case letter is simply a smaller form of the capital. Neither has changed much in shape in the past 2,000 years.

D, d

The fourth letter of the alphabet since Semitic times, *D* derives from Greek *delta*, Δ. A right-rounded shape appeared in Latin, and this came into English. The lower-case letter is a development of the capital, written rapidly to produce a form with a lengthened upper stroke and a reduced, left-rounded lower element.

E,e

E was a consonant symbol in the Semitic alphabet, but was used as a vowel in Greek, one of its shapes emerging in Latin and eventually in English as the capital letter. The lower-case letter developed as a smaller, rounded variant of the capital in a cursive style of handwriting.

F,f

F, along with *U*, *V* and *W*, comes from a single symbol used in the North Semitic alphabet. This gave rise to two letters in early Greek, one of which was adopted by the Etruscans and Romans. The elongated lower-case form arose later, when scribes began to run letters together in handwriting.

G,g

G is found first in the 4th century BC, in a revised version of the Latin alphabet. Previous alphabets had used the *C* symbol for the *g* sound (as in *god*), and the new symbol was a simple adaptation of that, adding a small crossbar. The lower-case form went through a complex set of changes to produce the modern symbols – the g with a closed lower element, as usually seen in print, and the 'open *g*' of handwriting.

H,h

H was originally a Semitic letter which came into Latin via Greek and Etruscan to represent the /h/ sound. The lower-case rounded form arose with the development of handwriting.

I,i

I was a consonant in the Semitic alphabet, represented a vowel in Greek, and came into Latin with both vowel and consonant values. The lower-case letter is a smaller form of the capital. The dot was originally a small diacritic, similar to an acute accent, added in early Middle English to distinguish the stroke of an *i* from the otherwise identical strokes of adjacent letters (*m, n, u*).

J,j

The history of this letter in English dates only from the medieval period. Originally a graphic variant of *i* (a lengthened form with a bottom left-facing curve), it gradually came to replace *i* whenever that letter represented a consonant, as in *jewel*. The lower-case distinction did not become standard until the mid-17th century, and there was uncertainty about the upper-case distinction even as late as the early 19th century.

K,k

K was a Semitic letter which came into Latin via Greek and Etruscan. It was little used in Latin (which preferred *C* and *Q*), and it is uncommon in Old English. The lower-case form arose in handwriting through a simple extension of the upright stroke above the line.

L,l

L was a symbol in the Semitic alphabet, and developed via Greek, Etruscan and Latin into the modern capital form, with a horizontal line replacing an earlier oblique. The lower-case letter arose in handwriting, when scribes joined *L* to adjacent letters by using an upper loop and turning the horizontal stroke into a curve. These linking features were omitted in the printed form.

M,m

M has come from a Semitic letter via the Greek, Etruscan and Latin alphabets (where it sometimes had four vertical strokes) into Old English. The lower-case letter appeared in a rounded form in handwriting.

N,n

N achieved its present-day shape in the Latin alphabet after a history of various angular forms. The rounded lower-case letter resulted from scribal handwriting practice. It appears in Old English, and has been used with very little change in form since.

O,o

O represented a consonant in the Semitic alphabet, and was used by the Greeks for both a short and a long vowel, these later being distinguished as two symbols, *omicron* ('little o', for the short sound) and *omega* ('big o', for the long sound). The Romans adopted omicron, giving it both short and long values, and these values were also assigned to the letter when it was used in Old English. The lower-case letter is a smaller form of the capital.

P,p

P was a Semitic letter which came into Greek, Etruscan and Latin in a variety of forms. It eventually standardised with a rounded upper element. The lower-case letter is a smaller version of the capital, with the additional distinction that the vertical stroke falls below the line of writing.

Q,q

The location of the distinctive stroke has varied greatly from the Semitic alphabet through Greek and Etruscan to Latin, until a curved 'tail' at the bottom and to the right of the *O* became the standard form. The letter was dropped in Classical Greek, but retained in Etruscan as the representation of /k/ before a *u* vowel, and this practice was taken over in Latin. The lower-case letter developed in scribal writing as a smaller version of the capital, with the tail lengthened below the line and moved to the right, to facilitate rapid script.

R,r

R appeared in the Semitic alphabet in a variety of forms, and was taken into Greek with a single descending stroke. A version with an additional short 'tail' became the basis of the Latin form, with the tail lengthened to avoid confusion with *P*. The lower-case form arose as a simplified character in handwriting, with the curve and tail smoothed into a single wavy horizontal stroke.

S,s

The Semitic and Greek alphabets had a variety of symbols for *s*-like (*sibilant*) sounds, one of which – a rounded form – was taken over by the Etruscans and Romans and eventually entered Old English, usually written in an elongated way. The lower-case letter is simply a smaller version of the capital, though a form resembling an *f* (but without the cross-bar) came to be used in handwriting in the 17th century, and is found in print until the early 19th century.

T,t

T was used in the Semitic alphabet, came into Latin via Greek and Etruscan, and entered Old English. The handwritten form was a smaller and rounded version of the capital, with a right-curved base. The vertical stroke later became lengthened above the horizontal, forming a cross-bar, in order to distinguish the handwritten *t* from *c*.

U,u

The ancestor of *U* is to be found in the Semitic alphabet, eventually emerging in Latin as a *V* used for both consonant and vowel. The lower-case letter developed as a smaller and rounded form in handwriting. In Middle English, both *v* and *u* appear variously as consonant and vowel, *v* often being found at the beginning of a word and *u* in the middle. This eventually led to *v* being reserved for the consonant and *u* for the vowel, though it was not until the late 17th century that this distinction became standard.

V,v

The history of this letter is the same as for *U*. Once a systematic distinction had emerged between the two letters, a larger version of *u* became standard as a capital, and a small version of *V* became standard as a lower-case form.

W,w

This letter was introduced by Norman scribes in the 11th century as a means of representing the sound /w/, replacing the runic letter which had been used in Old English. Although its shape is a ligature of two *v*s, its name is 'double u', reflecting the state of affairs in Middle English when *v* and *u* were interchangeable. The lower-case letter is a smaller version of the capital.

X,x

X emerged in the Greek alphabet, derived from an earlier Semitic sibilant letter. It came into Latin with the value of /ks/, and was used in Old English typically as a variant spelling of *cs*. The lower-case letter is a smaller version of the capital.

Y,y

Y is a Greek adaptation of a Semitic symbol. In Roman times, it was borrowed to help transcribe Greek loanwords into Latin. The rounded lower-case letter developed as part of handwriting, enabling scribes to write it in a single movement, The trunk of the letter was placed below the line, and moved to the right to enable a smoother link to be made with the following letter.

Z,z

Z appeared in the Semitic and Greek alphabets, and although it was not needed for Latin, the Romans later borrowed the symbol to help transcribe Greek loanwords, making it the last item in their alphabet. The lower-case form is a smaller version of the capital.

5

The basic weaknesses

*The Old English alphabet had several weaknesses: some
letters had more than one sound, and some sounds were
shown by more than one letter. These problem cases are
the source of several later spelling difficulties.*

In an ideal phonetic alphabet, each letter has just
one sound, and vice versa. But ten of the letters in
the Anglo-Saxon alphabet weren't like that. Three of
the problem cases were consonants.

The letter *h* was used to spell the breathed sound
at the beginning of a word, as in *hand* ('hand'), which
was pronounced much as it is today. It was also used
to spell a friction sound at the back of the mouth, in
such words as *miht* ('might'). We can hear that sound
today in the way Scottish people pronounce the last
sound in *loch,* and it can even be heard occasionally
in other accents, such as when people make a noise
of disgust, like *yuck,* but stretch the final sound.

The letter *c* was also used to spell two different
sounds. Both of them are still in use today: the hard,
plosive /k/ sound in *cold,* and the softer /tʃ/ sound
in *child.* Today the spelling shows the difference, but

in Old English the initial consonant letter was the same for both: *cald* ('cold') and *cild* ('child'). The choice often depended on the phonetic quality of the adjacent vowel sound, but the situation could still be confusing. The word for 'king', *cyning*, began with a /k/, as in the modern word, whereas the word for 'cheese', *cyse*, began with a /tʃ/. It was even worse with a word like *spræc*, which could be pronounced in two different ways: when it was the past tense of the verb *sprecan* ('speak') it had a /k/; when it was the noun meaning 'speech', it had a /tʃ/. How would an Anglo-Saxon reader know which sound to use? Some scribes must have realised there was a problem, because they experimented with various alternative spellings, such as by spelling *cyning* with a *k* – *kyning*. But the situation remained very uncertain. (Even today, we can find variation with this letter: is it *disc* or *disk*?)

The letter *g* was a particular problem as it was used to spell *three* different sounds. When it was followed by a consonant, as in *gnæt* ('gnat'), it had the hard, plosive /g/ sound of Modern English *go*. The same sound was heard if it was followed by a vowel made at the back of the mouth – *a*, *o*, or *u*, as in such words as *gar* ('spear'), *godspell* ('gospel') and *guma* ('man'). But if the following vowel was at the front of the mouth – *i*, *e*, *æ*, or *y* – then it was pronounced with a vowel-like /j/ sound, as in Modern English *yes*. So, *gif* ('if') was pronounced /jif/ and *gear* ('year') was pronounced with the consonant sound we still use today. And that's not all. When the *g* appeared after a back vowel, or between two back vowels, it had a third pronunciation – one which doesn't occur in Modern English, but which can be heard in Modern German in such words as *sagen* ('to say'). The closest we get to it in English today is in the sound at the end of *loch*, but with the vocal cords buzzing. So, when we see *fugol* ('fowl'), we need to know that the first syllable was not like Modern English *fug*, with a hard *g*, but a more relaxed, longer sound.

In these three cases, *h*, *c* and *g*, we see a consonant letter having more than one sound. This is a clear departure from the phonetic principle. And there were two cases of the opposite happening: a single consonant sound being written with more than one letter. Listen to the sound that occurs at the end of words like *hedge*: /ʤ/ in the list shown in Chapter 3. Scribes didn't know what to do about this. Some wrote it with a *g* – yet another sound for that letter! Some doubled it – *gg*. But most opted for a sequence of two letters, *c* and *g*. In which order? Usually *cg*; sometimes *gc*. So we find *hecg*, *secgan* ('say') and so on.

And listen to the sound that occurs at the beginning of such words as *ship* and *shove*: /ʃ/ in the list in Chapter 3. This they wrote with a combination of *s* + *c*, as in *scip* ('ship') and *scufan* ('shove'). But there was an additional problem with this spelling. The same pairing of *s* + *c* was also used to spell the sequence of sounds /s/ + /k/, as in *scolu* 'school'

and *Scotland*. How should *sc* be sounded – as /ʃ/ or
as /sk/? This would cause a lot of head-scratching in
later years.

So, to sum up the consonant situation: three
letters, *h*, *c* and *g*, were being used to spell a total of
seven sounds. And two letter-pairs, *cg* and *sc*, were
being used to spell one sound each. Moreover, *sc* was
being used to spell two different sound sequences.
None of this was good. It was a weakness, storing up
trouble for later on, as pronunciation changed and
new spelling fashions emerged.

An even greater weakness affected the vowels.
There were seven vowel letters in Old English – the
five we know today as *a*, *e*, *i*, *o* and *u*, plus ash (*æ*)
and *y*. This last one is still used as a vowel letter: we
see it in *my* and *rhyme*, for example. In Old English,
it represented a rounded sound at the front of the
mouth – like the vowel sound in French *tu* ('you') or
the way some Scottish people pronounce the vowel
in words like *look*. Now, if each of these letters had
represented just one sound, there would have been
no problem. But each had two: a short sound and a
long sound. The word for 'god' was spelled *god*, with
a short sound, just as it has today; however, the word
for 'good' was also spelled *god*, with a long sound
(/goːd/) – much as if we were saying 'goad' now.
Similarly, the word for 'hare' was spelled *hara*, with
a short sound, similar to *hat* today; but the same
spelling was used for *hara* with a long sound /ɑː/
('hahra'), meaning 'hoary'. Similar things happened

with the other vowels. We have a vestige of this problem still. How do we know that *hypocrite* has a short *y* sound and *hypodermic* has a long one? Only by knowing the words. The two values of the letter *y* remain a challenge.

The diphthongs – sounds containing two vowel qualities – presented a similar problem. It's actually very difficult to work out what these sounds were like in Old English, and exactly how many there were. But the scribes definitely used sequences of two vowel letters – most often *e* + *a* and *e* + *o*, sometimes *i* + *e* and others. We find many words spelled in this way, such as *healf* ('half') and *heorte* ('heart'). They must have had a distinctive force, as otherwise there would have been all kinds of misunderstanding. If we do the substitution exercise of Chapter 3, we find Old English had *beod* ('table') as well as *bed* ('bed') and *bod* ('command'). We find *leaf* ('leaf') as well as *lef* ('weak') and *laf* ('remainder'). Some of these words had a short sound for the first part of the diphthong and some had a long one. The length could change the meaning: *sceat* (/ʃɛət/), with a short first sound, meant 'property'; with a long first sound (/ʃɛːət/), it meant 'region'. This length difference no longer exists today, but we can get some idea of it if we take the modern word *there*, which contains a similar diphthong, and say it in a very abrupt, clipped tone of voice, and then in a very slow, sympathising way (*There, there!*).

How to tell the difference between a short and a

long vowel or diphthong when reading aloud? That must have been a real problem for the monks, if they were reading an unfamiliar text to a congregation. They had to get the pronunciation right. The obvious way to show the difference would be to mark the length on the vowel itself, perhaps by doubling (such as *aa*) or by using a diacritic (such as *à*). Several languages (such as Dutch) show vowel length by doubling: *a* vs. *aa*, *e* vs. *ee* and so on. And if, today, we wanted to show a really long sound in English, that's how we'd do it: *argh, aargh, aaargh* – the more disgusted we feel, the more *a*s we use (Chapter 34). It feels like a natural way of representing the length of a sound, and some Anglo-Saxon scribes did actually experiment with double letters. In an early glossary, we find the word for the weapon 'pike' spelled *piic* (/piːk/) and the word for 'mouse' spelled *muus* (/muːs/) But this way of spelling never caught on at the time. These words eventually came to be spelled *pic* and *mus*. Today, of course, we use doubling a lot to show a long vowel sound, as in *feet* and *fool*; but we still don't feel entirely comfortable with it, for we don't use it with all the vowels – no *aa*, *ii* or *uu*, apart from in a few very exotic words (such as *aardvarks*, *shiitake* mushrooms and *muumuu* dresses). Far more common is to use a combination of two different vowel letters to show a long vowel sound, as in *sea, lie, hoe, great* and so on. We'll look at these in Chapter 6.

Some scribes experimented with diacritics too,

marking a long vowel with an accent, such as *mús* ('mouse') and *hús* ('house'), but this strategy never caught on either. Perhaps this was because marks over a letter were already being used with different functions. They sometimes showed that a word had been abbreviated – for example, *dryhten* ('lord') might be written *drhyt̄*. And sometimes marks showed the way the voice should rise or fall when reading aloud, a bit like the way we use a question-mark today. But whatever the reason, the scribes didn't go down the diacritic road to solve their vowel length problem.

Despite the best of intentions, the monks devised an alphabet with real weaknesses. Ten of the twenty-seven letters were not being used in a straightforwardly phonetic way – the seven vowels and three of the consonants. It probably wasn't a great problem for them. The total number of words in Old English was relatively small (*c.* 50,000), and the range of subject-matter was relatively limited, compared to today. In cases like the two meanings of *sceat*, mentioned above, the context would probably have made it clear which sense was intended. This is, after all, what we do today with such pairs of words as *lead* ('to conduct') and *lead* ('a mineral') or *minute* ('unit of time') and *minute* ('very small'). It's rare to be confused. And if, when reading a text, a monk was momentarily stumped by a spelling, he always had the option of 'marking up' his text in some way, as a reminder.

But this situation could last only as long as the Anglo-Saxons continued to pronounce their words in the same way. And pronunciation never stands still. Over the next four centuries, major changes took place in the way English spoken vowels and consonants worked. Spelling had to adapt, if it was going to keep up with these changes.

Hope for us all

School reports of the winner of the 1953 Nobel Prize for Literature, at the end of his first school term in 1882, when he was eight:

> Writing and spelling: Writing good but so slow – spelling weak.

In the summer term:

> Writing good but so terribly slow – spelling as bad as it well could be.

But by 1884:

> Writing and spelling: Both much improved.

(From Randolph S. Churchill, *Youth: Winston S. Churchill, 1874–1900*, 1966, p.50–52.)

6
Keeping things long

Because English is a language where words often depend on the length of a vowel sound for their identity, one of the most urgent tasks facing the early writers was to show the difference between a short and a long vowel in the spelling. Various strategies were available to show the long vowels.

The Anglo-Saxon era in English history came to an end with the Norman invasion of 1066. Old English continued to be written until around 1150, but slowly evolved a new linguistic identity, known as Middle English. It is a development characterised by major changes in grammar, vocabulary, pronunciation and spelling. Thousands of new words entered the language from French and Latin. By the end of the Middle English period (*c.*1450) the size of the English lexicon would have doubled to around 100,000 items. The pressure on the scribes was greater than it had ever been before. Each of these new words had to be spelled.

The vowel length problem must have been an early priority, and there seemed to be two basic ways of solving it. The scribes could do something to show that a vowel was long – or they could do something to show that it was short. In the end, they did both, and we continue to use their two strategies today. The 'long vowel' solution was to add a 'silent' *e*: *hop* is short, and *hope* is long. The 'short vowel' solution was to double the next consonant: *hopping* has a short vowel sound, and *hoping* has a long one.

Sound out the difference between *hop* and *hope*, *hopping* and *hoping*, *sit* and *site*, *sitting* and *siting*. In each case, the silent letter *e* is the clue that the preceding vowel sound is long, and the double consonant letter is the clue that the preceding vowel sound is short. These are two of the basic principles of English spelling. It's the automatic way in which a modern speller would interpret an unfamiliar word. If I invent a word for a new kind of activity, and spell it *snopping*, you would say it with a short sound, and know that it comes from *to snop*. But if I spell it *snoping*, you'd say it with a long sound, and know that it comes from *to snope*. You'd also know that people who *snope* are called *snopers*, whereas those who *snop* are called *snoppers*.

Why couldn't the first Anglo-Saxon monks have used these strategies as a way of solving their problems? Because every letter was pronounced in Old English. If there was a vowel letter at the end of a word, it would be sounded: *hete* ('hate') was pronounced /hetə/ – 'het-uh'. So it couldn't be used as a 'silent' letter. And the same point applied to consonant doubling. If a consonant was doubled it would sound twice as long: *biddan* ('to pray') had a much longer 'd' than *bidan* ('to wait'). (It's a bit like what happens in Modern English when we say *nightie*, with a single /t/, and *night-time*, with a lengthened /t:/.) But if all vowel and consonant letters are being pronounced, then they can't be used as a technique to sort out spelling problems.

This situation altered as the Old English period came to an end. There were many subsequent changes in pronunciation. One of them was that the inflections of Old English – the word-endings which showed how words related to each other in a sentence – gradually died out, so that the *-e* letter in words like *hete* was no longer pronounced. Another was that people stopped pronouncing long consonants. Once this happened, the scribes must have realised that they could put the 'extra' letters to good use. So they started using *e* to show that the preceding vowel sound was long, as in *hope*, and a two-consonant spelling to show that the preceding vowel sound was short, as in *hopping*. In some cases they found that they didn't even have to change the spellings. If there already was an *e*, as in *hate*, they simply kept it. And a word like Old English *biddan* ('ask'), with a short vowel sound and a long consonant sound, slipped naturally into Middle English *bidden*, with a short vowel sound and a short consonant sound. However, there were also many cases where the spelling continued to be variable or unclear, so something more systematic needed to be done. The story of Modern English spelling really starts here.

How to show a long vowel? The scribes were faced with the same problem we have today when we hear an unfamiliar word for the first time and have to write it down. How would you write this made-up word, here shown in phonetic transcription: /fu:p/? There are several possibilities, such as *foop*, *foup* and *fupe*. All three methods do the job: double the letter; combine two letters; add a silent *e*. And from the 12th century, it's clear that scribes used them all. We find *moon* spelled as *moon*, *moun* and *mone*; *name* as *naam*, *naym* and *name*; *queen* as *queen*, *quean* and *quene*. Some spellings used two of the methods at the same time: we find *moone* and *moune*, *naame* and *nayme*, *queene* and *quiene*.

It's not possible to predict which method would eventually be used for a particular word. A lot must have depended on the other words that scribes brought to mind when they were thinking about what to do. For example, hearing the word for a new type of fish in the 15th century, they might have spelled its name in several ways, such as *hake*, *heak*, *haak* and *haik*. We actually do find *haake* among the first recorded attempts to write the word down. But the rhyme with such words as *bake*, *make*, *take* and *sake* must have been influential, as soon *hake* was the only spelling in use.

We continue to think in this way today. In deciding how to write /fu:p/ we mentally compare it with other words we know, such as *coop, soup* and *dupe*. Of course, these days we would simply look an unknown word up in a dictionary, and hope to find it there. That's one of the main uses people make of their dictionaries: to check on spelling. But in the 12th century there were no English dictionaries and the first attempts to compile spelling lists didn't appear until 400 years later. The scribes were on their own.

Thanks to the changes in pronunciation between Old and Middle English, the 'silent' *e* was emerging as the favourite way of marking a long vowel. We see it now, especially when there is a preceding *a* or *i*: for example in *name, tale, gate, safe, page, base ... side, wife, like, mile, time, mice ...* But there are examples of a silent *e* showing length in relation to all the vowel letters: *these, theme, scene, swede, glebe ... rode, yoke, hole, home, nose ... rude, lute, duke, rule, June.*

However, a 'silent' *e* strategy couldn't solve all instances of long vowels. It couldn't be used if there was no final consonant, for a start. How to write words like *tree*? And it evidently didn't apply to all words, for today we have *queen* not *quene*. As those examples illustrate, the French scribes evidently favoured a second way of marking length: doubling – at least for some vowels. Old English scribes hadn't liked double letters, as we saw in Chapter 5, but their French counterparts were clearly very happy to use *ee* and we see it now in many words, such as *tree, queen, seek, thee, sleep, seed* and *sweet*.

They avoided doubling for *i* and *u*, because *ii* and *uu* spellings would be very difficult to read (as we'll see in Chapter 15). And *aa* never survived, probably because the 'silent' *e* spelling had more quickly established itself as the norm, as in *name, tale,* etc. There are examples of *aa* spellings for several of these words in early Middle English, but they soon died out. Today such spellings are rare, seen in just a few loanwords where the spelling reflects a long vowel in the source language, as in *aardvark, bazaar* and *naan* (bread).

That leaves *oo*. Words spelled with *ee* are nice and regular today: *seek* rhymes with *meek, see* with *fee* and so on. No exceptions. But words with *oo* are quite the opposite: *boot* does not rhyme with *foot,* in most accents; *good* does not rhyme with *blood*. So what has happened here? In Old English, these words all had long vowels: *foot* was pronounced 'foht' /foːt/, *good* was 'gohd' /goːd/, and *blood* was 'blohd' /bloːd/. What happened is that in some cases the long vowel remained (which is why we have *moon, school, food,* etc.), and in some cases it shortened – in the south of England becoming *look, good, wool, foot,* etc. The vowel stayed with lip-rounding in these instances. In the case of *blood* and *flood,* the long vowel shortened and the lip-rounding disappeared too. But in all cases the *oo* spelling remained, so that now these spellings reflect a pronunciation of a thousand years ago.

The rider 'in the south of England' is important.

In several modern accents, such as in the north of England and in Scotland, the long-vowel pronunciation of words like *look* and *good* is still to be heard. In such places *boot* does rhyme with *foot*, and sometimes regional spelling draws attention to the difference, as with Scottish *guid* instead of *good*.

So now we have two ways of marking a long vowel: 'silent' *e* and doubling. We might think that ought to be enough. But neither of these strategies handled a third type of problem, which had arisen because of the way pronunciation had changed between Old and Middle English. And this has left us with one of the biggest spelling pains of today: *see* and *sea*, *piece* and *peace*. Why are these different?

The short answer is that these pairs once had different pronunciations. The vowel in *piece* sounded like a long version of the vowel we hear in the Received Pronunciation of Modern English *pay*. It is made with the front of the tongue quite high in the mouth: /pe:s/. The vowel in *peace* sounded like a long version of the vowel we hear in *pair*. It is made with the tongue lower and the mouth more open: /pɛ:s/. We can feel and hear the difference if we say *pay* and *pair* quickly in sequence. *Piece* and *peace* wouldn't be confused in speech, of course, but in writing there was a problem. One scribe might think the best way of writing the 'piece' word was *peece*; another might think that the best way of writing the 'peace' word was *peece*. Or they might both be written as *pese*, or *peyse*, or some other form. All these spellings have been recorded. There was therefore a real need to distinguish the two words.

The scribes hit on an ingenious solution. They sensed that the vowel in *piece* was close to other vowels made high in the front of the mouth, which were often spelled with a letter *i*. We hear this /iː/ quality today spelled as *i* in such words as *police* and *intrigue*. So, some scribes took the 'peece' spelling and put an *i* in front of the *e*: *piece*. Similarly, they sensed that the vowel of *peace* was close to other vowels made low in the front of the mouth, which were often spelled with a letter *a*, as in *man*. So, they took the 'peece' spelling and replaced the second *e* with an *a*: *peace*. Job done. And the idea caught on. It wasn't necessary to change both words, of course. Just changing one of them would make the difference nicely – which is why we find such pairs as *see* and *sea*, *meet* and *meat* or *reed* and *read*.

The three strategies were able to cope with virtually all the cases of long vowels that the scribes encountered. But inevitably, the system had to be tweaked, to keep pace with changes in the language. For example, the adverb *too* (as in *We went there too*) had developed out of the preposition *to* in Anglo-Saxon times, and was originally spelled in the same way – *to*. But this was confusing: *to much charity* could be read as 'to much charity' or 'too much charity'. And so the practice grew in the 16th century of spelling the adverb with a double vowel.

This well reflected the stress pattern of the two

words: *to* is usually unstressed; *too* is stressed. And the feeling that doubled vowels reflected a stressed syllable, whereas a single vowel reflected an unstressed syllable, accounts for some other spelling practices of the time. *Me,* for instance, is sometimes stressed (as in *Give it to me*) and sometimes unstressed (as in *Give me a chance*). So we find it spelled both as *mee* and *me*. Sometimes we even see both in the same sentence, such as in this line from the King James Bible (Ruth 1:20): *Call me not Naomi; call mee Mara.* The version with a double letter eventually died out. People must have tired of writing two letters when one would do, in such a frequently used word.

A few other common words received the same treatment, and explain some of the anomalies we notice today. *Do* also has both a stressed and an unstressed form (*I do hope so, Do I know you?*), and *doo, doe* and *do* are all found until *do* prevails in the 16th century. *So* has a long vowel, so we might expect it to be spelled *soo*. It did have this spelling for a while, but the shorter form came out on top. Frequency is inevitably a factor when it comes to spelling. People are always ready to find ways of shortening the most frequently used words – a process we still see in operation today in abbreviations such as *c* ('see') and *u* ('you') in text-messaging.

The also has two forms (unstressed in *That's the one,* and stressed, in its sense of pre-eminent, in *That's* the *textbook to use*), and we do find the spelling *thee* in Middle English alongside *the*. But the frequent use of the pronoun *thee* ('you') made it unlikely that the doubled form would last, and *the* quickly became the norm. It's quite common to see an unusual spelling arise because of the need to keep a later arrival in the language distinct from an earlier one, especially if the earlier usage is frequent. *Toe* was spelled both *too* and *toe* in Middle English, but the greater presence of *too* would have motivated the use of the *toe* spelling for the foot appendage. *Stake* was established in its modern spelling by the 14th century, so when the strip of meat arrived in the 15th, it needed a different spelling. We see writers experimenting with *steike*, *steyke*, *styke*, *steke* and *steake*, until eventually *steak* prevailed – a surprising result, given that the *ea* spelling was much more often used to represent the /i:/ sound, as in *speak*. The only *-eak* word which rhymes with *steak* is *break*.

There are many other examples of a word coming to be spelled in a particular way because of the existence of a prior word with which it might be confused. We'll see another example, *cloze*, in Chapter 14, and many instances when we discuss brand-names in Chapter 30. Grammar can be a factor too. The verb *curse* was spelled *curs* in Old English and kept that spelling in Middle English. Then, in the 14th century, along comes *cur* ('dog'), spelled *curre* but also *cur*. Once again, the shorter form was preferred. But when this word came to be used in the plural – quite a common occurrence, when servants or soldiers were being harangued (*you curs!*) – there was a clash. The solution was to add an *e* to make *curse* – something that would be needed anyway when the word was in the plural (*curses*).

How to spell long vowels is half of the story of vowel length. The other half is to see how the scribes coped with the short vowels. That story takes longer to tell.

More than letters

One day Polynesia and I were talking in the library. This was a fine long room with a grand mantelpiece and the walls were covered from the ceiling to the floor with shelves full of books: books of stories, books on gardening, books about medicine, books of travel; these I loved – and especially the Doctor's great atlas with all its maps of the different countries of the world.

This afternoon Polynesia was showing me the books about animals which John Dolittle had written himself.

'My!' I said, 'what a lot of books the Doctor has – all the way around the room! Goodness! I wish I could read! It must be tremendously interesting. Can you read, Polynesia?'

'Only a little,' said she. 'Be careful how you turn those pages – don't tear them. No, I really don't get time enough for reading – much. That letter there is a K and this is a B.'

'What does this word under the picture mean?' I asked.

'Let me see,' she said, and started spelling it out. 'B-A-B-O-O-N – that's monkey. Reading isn't nearly as hard as it looks, once you know the letters.'

(Hugh Lofting, 'My schoolmaster, Polynesia', from *The Voyages of Dr Dolittle*, 1922, Ch. 11)

7

Keeping things short

*The first writers of English had to show that words
contained a short vowel sound. Their basic principle was
to double the following consonant.*

What is the best way of showing that a vowel in an
English word is short? In around 1200, an English
monk named Orrm worked out a solution. Based at
one of the monasteries in the East Midlands, he is
known for a single work, the *Orrmulum*, a collection
of thirty-two homilies intended for church reading.
Orrm was in no doubt that preachers needed help
when reading aloud. In particular, he knew they
needed clues to tell when a vowel sound was long
and when it was short. So he decided to reform the
spelling system. He decided that the best way to help
was to rely totally on a consonant-doubling principle. If a word had a short vowel, then the following
consonant would be doubled. And he carried this
principle through his entire work with remarkable
consistency.

The result didn't seem to impress. Nobody
adopted his system, and the *Orrmulum* remains a

glorious idiosyncrasy. It was indeed a much more regular approach to spelling English, but it couldn't have been easy to read or economical to write. Words dramatically increase in length – 'sit' becomes *sitt*, 'after' becomes *affterr*, 'into english' is *inntill ennglissh*. There are hundreds of punchy monosyllables with a short vowel in English, often just two, three or four letters in length: *up, in, cat, bid, dog, stop, rob, ram, tin* ... It's one of the main features of the language. In Orrm's system they would all be *upp, catt, dogg* and so on. It would take a scribe a lot longer to write something out in Orrm's system. Labour-saving it wasn't – and it just didn't appeal.

The basic idea was sound enough, though: doubling is useful. We need a way of telling the difference between *hoping* from *hopping*, as we saw in the previous chapter. But evidently scribes felt they shouldn't overdo it. We'll never know exactly how they worked it out, but eventually a set of strategies evolved. They seem to have wanted a kind of spelling minimalism: avoid heavy-looking spellings. So, keep those words like *rob* and *dog* nice and short. These were rapidly increasing in number, in the early Middle Ages, because of an influx of Scandinavian loanwords: *get, leg, kid, cut, hit* ... They included some of the commonest words in the language. How they were to be treated would have a fundamental impact on the graphic character of English.

Not everyone took the minimalist point straight away. Even in Old English, some short words had been spelled in two ways – *catt* and *cat,* for example – and in the Middle English period we continue to find such variants as *dogg* and *dog,* or *ratt* and *rat.* In some cases, the shorter spelling wasn't established until the 16th century. But eventually the simpler spellings did prevail for an important set of words – those ending in *p, b, t, d, g, m* and *n* – letters which represent the plosive ('hard') and nasal consonant sounds. It's very unusual for these sounds to be shown with a doubled consonant, though we do find a few modern examples, especially in names (*Chubb, Finn, Lapp*) and some exotic loanwords, such as *djinn.* Words like *watt, mitt* and *mutt* look like exceptions, until we remember how they arose: *watt* is from a name (*James Watt*), and *mitt* and *mutt* are shortened forms (*mitten, muttonhead*).

Note that letter *k* is missing from the list of letters representing plosive sounds. It had never been much used in Old English, and perhaps the sight of a *kk* didn't appeal to the Norman scribes either, for the spelling that came to be used for the /k/ sound after a short vowel was *ck.* That's why today we find *baking* distinguished from *backing,* never *bakking.*

The scribes must have sensed a difference between the above sounds and the 'friction' consonant sounds spelled with *f, s* and *z,* as well as the 'liquid' sounds spelled with *l* and *r,* because they kept the double consonant in these cases. That's why we have *cliff, ruff, doff, stuff, sniff; kiss, toss, fuss, mess, lass; ill, spell, skull, doll, tell; burr, purr, whirr.* Words ending in -z were rare at the time (*buzz*), but later words followed the same pattern: *fizz, jazz*. Here too there was some vacillation for a while: we find *ruff* alongside *ruf, lass* and *las, tell* and *tel, buzz* and *buz*. And most of the words ending in *rr* were later simplified, so that words like *carr, blurr* and *torr* are now spelled *car, blur* and *tor*. Pronunciation changed in some accents, too, with final *r* no longer being pronounced, so that the vowel sounds in these words are now long. That can cause uncertainty even today: is it *whirr* or *whir*? *burr* or *bur*? We'll find both.

The scribes seemed to have left the 'little' words alone – the grammatical words which show the structure of a sentence, such as *on, in, up, if, of* and *at*. They all have short vowels, so it would have been logical to double the consonant, as Orrm did. Some Old English scribes indeed wrote such forms as *inn* and *upp*, and there are examples of doubling in Middle English too, but the vast majority of spellings retained the single consonant letter, as they do today. *Off* is an exception, but that word originates as a variant of the word *of*, and the extra letter was needed to distinguish the two meanings, as in *of course* vs. *off course*.

So, the principle seems straightforward: double a letter only when you have to, such as when you add an ending or to avoid two words looking the same. That's why we see *batting* distinguished from *bating*, *ridding* from *riding*, *pinning* from *pining*, *robber* from *rober*, *inn* from *in* and so on. It took several hundred years for this principle to work its way through the system, but its importance was clearly appreciated. New words coming into English from French followed it. When French *bagage* arrived in the 15th century, English speakers shifted the stress from the French pattern *bagage*, to the first, *bagage*, and then doubled the consonant to show the vowel was short, *baggage*. That's why we have *bonnet, cabbage, jolly* and many more.

We see signs of this principle everywhere: don't overdo it. Yes, double the consonant after a word like *pin*, to produce *pinning*, but if the short vowel sound was already being spelled with two vowel letters – then don't double. So that meant writing *sweating* not *sweatting*, *threading* not *threadding*, *cooker* not *cookker*, *trouble* not *troubble* and so on. There aren't many such spellings, as usually two vowel letters represent a long vowel sound, as we saw in Chapter 6, but pronunciation had changed between Old and Middle English, and some of the words that had diphthongs in Old English became single vowels later, though they kept the earlier spelling. *Bread* was pronounced /brɛːəd/ in Old English – similar to the sound we hear in the Received Pronunciation of *fair* today – but by Middle English the diphthong had gone, and the word was pronounced much as it is now. However, the old two-letter spelling stayed.

The same sort of desire to keep the spelling looking as light as possible motivated a second strategy: don't double a consonant-letter after a short

vowel if there are already two consonants representing two sounds. This was a very common pattern in
English – two consonant sounds at the end of a word,
as in *want, jump, soft, risk, wind* and many more. So
that meant writing *wanting,* not *wannting, wantting* or
wanntting; and similarly *jumping, softer, risky, window,
sister* ... I suppose they thought like this: *nt* in *want*
is already a sort of doubling, so let's leave that as the
signal for the short vowel.

So far, so good. We have a straightforward principle of doubling with just a few easy-to-follow and
sensible adaptations. But it didn't stay that way. The
Normans had different ideas.

Spelling as tragedy

'I don't think any tragedy in literature that I have ever come across impressed me so much as the first one, that I spelled out slowly for myself in words of three letters: the bad fox has got the red hen. There was something so dramatically complete about it; the badness of the fox, added to all the traditional guile of his race, seemed to heighten the horror of the hen's fate, and there was such a suggestion of masterful malice about the word 'got.' One felt that a countryside in arms would not get that hen away from the bad fox. They used to think me a slow dull reader for not getting on with my lesson, but I used to sit and picture to myself the red hen, with its wings beating helplessly, screeching in terrified protest, or perhaps, if he had got it by the neck, with beak wide agape and silent, and eyes staring, as it left the farmyard for ever. I have seen blood-spillings and down-crushings and abject defeat here and there in my time, but the red hen has remained in my mind as the type of helpless tragedy.

(Spoken by Tom Kerlway, in H. H. Munro, *The Unbearable Bassington*, 1912, Ch. 8)

8

The first exceptions

*The French scribes introduced several exceptions to the
doubling principle for showing short vowels. Several
problems arose as a result.*

Many of our modern spelling conventions origi-
nate with the writing habits of the Norman French
scribes. The incomers had no interest in preserving
the distinctive Anglo-Saxon letters, such as thorn
(þ) and eth (ð), with all their Germanic associations,
and they quickly replaced them by *th*. They didn't
like the Anglo-Saxon use of *sc* to spell /ʃ/, so they
replaced it with *sh*, as in *ship*. They distinguished the
two uses of letter *c* described in Chapter 5 – *cald* and
cild – spelling the latter as *child*, as today. The *cw* of
words like *cwen* was replaced by *qu*, a spelling well
known from both French and Latin writing. The *h* in
words like *miht* (representing the 'loch' sound) was
replaced by *gh*, as in *might*. They weren't quite sure
what to do with the consonant sound at the end of
words like *hedge* /dʒ/: the Anglo-Saxon *cg* lasted for a
while, competing with *gg*, until eventually *dg* took
over. They kept *ng* to spell the consonant sound at

the end of words like *sing*. In later chapters I'll look more fully at what these French scribes did (Chapters 11–13).

This set of innovations presented writers with something of a problem, when it came to applying the minimalist doubling principle to show a short vowel. If a consonant sound was already being spelled with two letters, to double it to show a short vowel would mean that there would be four. This would result in spelling *moth* as *moththt*, *fishing* as *fishshing* and so on. Nobody liked that. And so another strategy was established: don't double if a sound is already spelled with two letters.

We do find occasional doublings, such as *moththe* and *fishshe*, in medieval manuscripts, but they plainly weren't popular. And something extra happened to *ch*. To begin with, we find examples of doubling: *hachch* ('hatch') and *machch* ('match'). Some writers then simplify: *hacch*, *macch*. But most followed the general trend, avoided doubling, and wrote *hach* and *mach*. It might have stayed that way, if the printers hadn't had other ideas (Chapter 19). Although William Caxton and the others left most of these undoubled consonants alone, they evidently didn't like the *ch* spelling of the sound /tʃ/. They added a *t*. The result was *hatch*, *wretch* and all the other *-tch* spellings we have today.

But the story of doubling isn't over yet. A joined letter *w* (what had earlier been written as *uu*) had arrived with the Norman scribes, and this soon displaced the old Anglo-Saxon letter wynn (p). At the same time, they were making more use of letter *v*. The problem quickly became evident. If people started spelling words like *loving* and *having* as *lovving* and *havving*, there was a real risk of confusion. In handwriting, *lovving* could be mistaken for *lowing*. Solution? Make *v* another exception. And ever since, the language has avoided double *v* spellings – as in *glove, live, give, dove, have, above, active* and a few more. We see double *v* today in just a handful of modern colloquialisms, such as *divvy* (dividend), *navvy* (labourer), *flivver* (for a cheap car or plane) and *revving* (*an engine*), and in representations of local dialect, such as *bovver* ('bother').

Avoiding a double *v* seems like a good solution, but – as so often with spelling – a decision made for one part of the lexicon introduces complications for another part. The scribes also had to solve the problem of distinguishing *u* and *v*, which looked identical in handwriting. Faced with a spelling that looked like *lou*, was this to be read as *low* or *love*? They decided to add a final *e*, which they thought would help to show that the *v* is a consonant. It didn't seem to bother them that a final *e* was already being used to mark a long vowel. So words like *give* and *above* ended up in their modern form. Only a very few words, mainly recent foreign loans, are spelled with a final *v*, as in *Slav, Molotov* (*cocktail*), *chav* and *Kalashnikov* (its use in children's books is discussed in Chapter 30).

We can see the origins of one of the modern spelling irritations now. The adjective *live* (as in *live animals*) has a long vowel, following the regular spelling rule. The verb *live* (as in *to live*) has a short vowel, following the exceptional marking of letter *v*. Similarly, Americans have to cope with the short vowel of *dove* the bird coexisting with the long vowel in the past tense of *dive* (*I dove into the pool*). Words ending in *ve* with a short vowel are not a big problem, as very few words are affected. But they are a nuisance, nonetheless, as some of the exceptional cases are frequently used in the language (*have*, especially), and so the exception is often before our eyes.

And there was yet another exception: the letter *x*. In Old English this had always been used to spell the two-consonant sound of /ks/ as in *ox*, *axe* and so on. These words had short vowels, so the logic of doubling meant that they should be spelled *oxx* and *axx*. It must have been the double sound in *x* that put people off, for these spellings were never used. We don't see them at all today – unless you want to form a pop group (*The Voxx, Bubba Sparxxx*), name a pharmaceutical (*Vioxx, Lexxel*), or spell words in a language from outer space. Then *xx* is an ideal choice, as it looks really alien. A being called *Vexxiz* is definitely from a universe far far away. (So are beings whose names contain a *ww*, *jj* and *hh*, as these are never doubled in English either. The only time we see two *h*s next to each other is when two words are combined to form a compound, and then we usually insert a hyphen to keep them apart, as in *bath-house*, rather than *bathhouse*.)

What with *up*, *cat*, *love* and *axe*, and all the other words where a single consonant follows a short vowel, we might find it easier to think of the doubling principle the other way round. Not: a short vowel sound is shown by a following double consonant. Rather: a long vowel sound is *never* shown by a following double consonant. This is actually a much better way of putting it, as it has far fewer exceptions. But unfortunately there are still a few. The friction and liquid sounds we encountered in Chapter 7 continue to cause trouble. There was uncertainty about what to do if a word had a long vowel sound and ended in *l*: *mole* and *hole*, *hale* and *vale*, *mile* and *pile* and many more eventually followed the 'silent letter' route; but *droll*, *roll*, *stroll*, *toll*, *all*, *call*, *wall*, *small* and several others ended up with doubling. Also, there are a very few cases where a long vowel is followed by a single consonant, without any silent *e* – they're all exotic loanwords, such as *khan* (the title, as in *Aga Khan*) and *nan* (bread), and the occasional plural form, such as *bras*.

A further set of exceptions to the 'never have two consonant letters after a long vowel' principle came about following an unusual development in the 18th century. This was the century in which usage was strongly influenced by class distinction: upper-class people in Britain did not want to talk like middle-class or working-class people, and by the end of the century the prestige accent of Received Pronunciation had emerged. Its speakers distinguished themselves by avoiding some of the features common in 'lower' speech – for example, they pronounced *h* if it was there in the spelling (*harm*, not *'arm*), and they avoided sounding an /r/ after a vowel (/fɑː/ for *far*). And they elongated some of their vowels. Not for them the short vowel in words like *bath* and *rather*, *class* and *grass*, *off* and *cross*. These vowels became long – 'bahth' (/bɑːθ/), 'grahss' (/grɑːs/), 'orff' (/ɔːf/) – and they remain a feature of the prestige accent to this day. But the result has been another group of exceptions, as far as spelling is concerned, for here again we have long vowel sounds followed by doubled consonants. The English spelling system thus represents regional accents which keep these vowels short in a much more regular way. It's sometimes easier to learn English spelling if you *don't* speak with Received Pronunciation.

The two principles we've been exploring are 'double a consonant' (the norm to show a preceding short vowel) and 'add a silent *e*' (the norm to show a preceding long vowel). It might be thought impossible to do both together, but nothing is impossible with spelling. And with a large number of later French loanwords we repeatedly see a double-consonant-plus-*e* (*CCe*) letter-combination at the end of a word – *brunette, gazelle, finesse, gavotte, omelette, cigarette* and many more. Not everyone fell in love with them. The shift of stress onto the first syllable in such words as *programme* and *kilogramme* prompted a respelling in American English (Chapter 26) – *program, kilogram* – and these spellings have begun to spread into British English too. *Program* is now the norm in computing everywhere.

All these *CCe* examples show a preceding short vowel sound. Could there ever be cases where *CCe* is used after a preceding long vowel? They're rare, but other French loanwords show some examples, such as *bizarre* and *mousse*. And Received Pronunciation gives us a further exception when speakers pronounce *giraffe* with a long *a*: /dʒɪrɑ:f/.

So, the English spelling system gives us a way of showing that a preceding vowel sound is short: double the following consonant (*hopping*). But bear in mind that there are three kinds of exception: sometimes we don't double (*cat*), sometimes we add an *e* (*love*), and sometimes we double *and* add an *e* (*cigarette*). We also have a way of showing that a preceding vowel sound is long: add a silent *e* (*mile*). But bear in mind that there are three kinds of exception: we sometimes don't use an *e* (*khan*), we sometimes double (*call*), and we sometimes double *and* add an *e* (*bizarre*).

You might think this has exhausted our list of exceptions to the short/long principles. You would be wrong.

9

Seeing the link

*Spelling is also able to show the relationship between the
basic form of a word and longer words derived from it
through the use of suffixes. However, this introduces still
more exceptions to the doubling principle.*

The whole point of spelling is to enable us to recognise words when they are written down. But there's
a second thing. We value spelling if it helps us to
recognise the relationship *between* words.

English builds words in a variety of ways. One of
the big things that happened in the Middle Ages was
a great increase in the number of prefixes and suffixes
– *con-, ex-, en-, -ance, -ity, -ment, -tion* and many more,
borrowed from French and Latin. Thousands of new
words were made by adding these elements to existing words – *light > lighten, enlighten, enlightenment* and
so on. And in many cases, the addition of a suffix
changed the pronunciation of a word. Listen to what
happens when we add an *-ic* or *-ical* ending to a word
with a long vowel sound: *type* becomes *typical*, *mime*
becomes *mimic*, *athlete* becomes *athletic*. In each case
the long vowel becomes short. It's a big problem for

learners: they have to know it's *tip-ical* not *tie-pical*. Consonants can be affected too: *sign* with a silent *g* becomes *signature* with the *g* pronounced.

Sometimes larger sets of words are involved. Listen to *telegraph, telegraphy, telegraphic,* and *telegraphese*. In *tele*graph we hear the stress on the first syllable; in *telegraphy* we hear it on the second syllable; in *telegraphic* we hear it on the third; and in *telegraphese* we hear it on the fourth. A consequence of this is that the vowels change their sound. So how are we to write them down? If we followed a strict phonetic principle, it would be something like this, with *u* representing the /ə/ sound of an unstressed vowel and *ah* showing the long vowel which is often heard in *telegraph*:

> telugrahph
> tulegruphy
> telugraphic
> telugruphese

These spellings make the words easy to pronounce – but at what cost? We have lost the visual identity between the four words. It's more difficult now to see that *telegraph* and *telegraphy* are basically 'the same'.

So here the medieval scribes and printers were faced with another choice: should they follow the sound or the sense? And they opted for the sense. They kept the spelling the same for the roots of the related words. Normally they would double a consonant letter after a short vowel sound, as we saw in Chapter 7. But they turned *crime* into *criminal*, not *crimminal*; *mime* into *mimic*, not *mimmic*; *type* into *typical*, not *typpical*. As more and more words came into the language, we see this principle extended to all such words, whatever the suffix: *sole* became *solitude*, not *sollitude*; *obscene* became *obscenity*, not *obscennity*; *cave* became *cavity* not *cavvity*. We do find some writers trying to follow the double-consonant principle: there are occasional spellings such as *mimmicke* and *sollitude*. But by the 16th century, the new principle was well established. *Electric? Electricity*, not *electriccity. Ferocious? Ferocity*, not *feroccity*. A whole new class of exceptions to the rule arrived.

The suffixes completely altered the look of English. Although there are only about fifty of them in everyday English, they appear in around half the words in the language. In technical and scientific English, the proportion is even greater. So the way suffixes are spelled, and the way they affect the spelling of the words to which they're attached, is of critical importance. And what happened, in the history of English, is that as the amount of borrowing from Latin increased, so the influence of the suffixes grew, altering the appearance of the orthography. The effect became really noticeable during the 16th century, when writers introduced thousands of obscure classical words into English. The practice was so controversial that they were called 'ink-horn' words (because they took a lot of ink to write) and many authors took pains to avoid them. But thousands of new words entered English nonetheless.

We see a good cross-section of these coinages in Robert Cawdrey's *Table Alphabeticall* of 1604 – the first attempt at an English dictionary. Its full title is *A Table Alphabeticall, conteyning and teaching the true writing, and vnderstanding of hard vsuall English wordes, borrowed from the Hebrew, Greeke, Latin, or French, &c.* For example, these are some of the words ending in *-itie* (modern *-ity*) that he lists under letter C: *calamitie, capacitie, carnalitie, celeritie, ciuilitie, clemencie, comentarie, concauitie*. We might expect all these short vowels to be followed by a double consonant – *ciuil-litie, concauuitie* and so on – but none are. The visual effect is very noticeable, because over half the words in his book have suffixes. And Cawdrey is in no doubt that his spelling is correct. In his dedication of the book to five 'worshipfull, vertuous, & godlie Ladies' of the English aristocracy, he describes his presentation as 'the true Orthography, that is, the true writing of many hard English words'.

Cawdrey did more than just list words, spellings and meanings. He actually taught people how to use such a book. In his address to the reader, he gives advice which today seems totally unnecessary; but in his day, looking a word up in a dictionary was beyond the experience of most users. So we read:

> If thou be desirous (gentle Reader) rightly and
> readily to vnderstand, and to profit by this Table,
> and such like, then thou must learne the Alphabet,

to wit, the order of the Letters as they stand,
perfectly without booke, and where euery Letter
standeth:

Not content with this, he adds an illustration:

as (b) neere the beginning, (n) about the middest,
and (t) toward the end.

And in case even this was not clear, he gives two
examples of the method:

Nowe if the word, which thou art desirous to
finde, begin with (a) then looke in the beginning
of this Table, but if with (v) looke towards the end.
Againe, if thy word beginne with (ca) looke in the
beginning of the letter (c) but if with (cu) then
looke toward the end of that letter. And so of all
the rest. &c.

Cawdrey also says something else in his dedication:
'And children heereby may be prepared for the understanding of a great number of Latine words: which
also will bring much delight & judgement to others.'

Latin as a source of 'delight and judgement'. By
judgement he means 'esteem', 'good opinion'. People
will approve if children use well-derived Latin words
– and, he might have added, spell them in a Latin
way.

Forensic spelling

[Poirot has found an envelope with some writing on it.]

'Tell me, how did those scribbled words on the envelope help you to discover that a will was made yesterday afternoon?'

Poirot smiled. 'Mon ami, have you ever, when writing a letter, been arrested by the fact that you did not know how to spell a certain word?'

'Yes, often. I suppose everyone has.'

'Exactly. And have you not, in such a case, tried the word once or twice on the edge of the blotting-paper, or a spare scrap of paper, to see if it looked right? Well, that is what Mrs. Inglethorp did. You will notice that the word "possessed" is spelt first with one "s" and subsequently with two – correctly. To make sure, she had further tried it in a sentence, thus: "I am possessed." Now, what did that tell me? It told me that Mrs. Inglethorp had been writing the word "possessed" that afternoon, and, having the fragment of paper found in the grate fresh in my mind, the possibility of a will – (a document almost certain to contain that word) – occurred to me at once.'

(Agatha Christie, *The Mysterious Affair at Styles*, 1920, Ch. 5)

10

Know your Latin and French

Latin was held in such reverence that writers wanted to spell English words as they were in Latin. This introduced still more exceptions to the doubling principle.

By the 16th century, Latin had come to be a language revered above all others. Who could match Roman writers for their elegance and style? And if English needed new words, where better a place to look? It was a state of mind which immediately affected English spelling, resulting in a new principle: if a word was spelled in a certain way in Latin, then it should be spelled in the same way in English.

This is a fine principle if you know Latin well. But if you don't, it's not much help. Today, it's no help at all to any but a few. Many of the exceptions to the double-consonant rule are due to the fact that the word is a Latin borrowing from this period, or a borrowing from Latin via French. And the same kind of attitude also affected words borrowed from Greek.

Take a word like *timid*, first used around 1550. If this had followed the doubling principle, it would be spelled *timmid*. But it was originally a Latin word, *timidus*, so writers spelled it with only one *m*, completely disregarding the traditional way of marking short vowels. And the same applied to other words ending in *-id*: *florid, acid, solid, vivid* ... Other Latinate suffixed words were handled similarly: *-ule* words, such as *schedule* (not *scheddule*), *module, nodule, granule, globule* ... Words ending in *-it* and *-et* were also kept single: *spirit, habit, profit; closet, comet, planet* ...

As earlier, some writers tried to introduce the doubling rule – we find *plannet* and *commet*, for example – but these were never favoured, presumably because they looked too English and not enough like Latin. Similarly, if a word had a double consonant in the original Latin, this too was kept. That's why we have *horrid, torrid, pallid, ferrule* and others. Again, it's the Latin appearance of these words that counted, it seems, not the fact that they happened to follow the doubling principle. And it didn't matter whether they came into English directly from Latin or indirectly via French.

The 'look' of a word is a serious point, and we see it clearly operating when we examine the way we spell words ending in *-ish*. Why do we spell *radish* with one *d* and *reddish* with two? It all depends where the words come from. In Old English, an *-ish* ending (spelled *-isc*) formed an adjective from the noun, meaning 'characteristic of', as in *Scottish* and *childish*, and this was used for other Germanic words later, so we get *reddish, doggish, oddish* and *mannish*. The consonant letter is doubled after the short vowel in these cases. But in the Middle Ages, a new group of words arrived from French, where the *-ish* ending was a respelling of a French verb ending containing an *s*, as in *punish, finish, abolish, perish* and dozens more, with the general meaning 'to initiate an action'. There's no consonant doubling in such cases. And similarly we have *pepper* (in Old English) with two *p*s and *leper* (from French) with one; or *copper* (in Old English) with two *p*s and *proper* (from French) with one.

As more and more words entered the language, the list of exceptions grew. *Canon* ('church law') is a good example. It arrived in English in Anglo-Saxon times, a loanword from Latin, spelled *canon*. During the Middle English period, scribes doubled the *n*, to mark the short vowel, but some writers must have felt that they needed to remember the Latin origins of the word, for they continued to spell it with a single *n*. Then the word for the gun arrived, a loanword from French, first recorded in 1588. This too was spelled in two ways: *canon* (following the French spelling) and *cannon* (following the short vowel principle). Given the substantial difference of meaning between the two words, there was very little risk of real ambiguity, but the desire to distinguish them grew as educated people began to support the notion of a 'correct spelling'. It could have gone either way. The uncertainty lasted until the 18th century, when Dr Johnson opted for *canon* (for the law) and *cannon* (for the weapon) – and what he decided to do carried enormous weight, as we'll see in Chapter 25.

So *cannon* follows the rule, and *canon* is the exception. Nor was it just Latin and French words that became exceptions. A few Anglo-Saxon words did too: although *body*, *shadow* and *widow* had spellings with two *d*s as well as one in the Middle Ages, they ended up with single consonant letters.

So, if you can tell your Latin and French sources from your Germanic ones, you'll know whether to double the consonant or not in most cases. If you don't, you've got a problem, and you're just going to have to learn these words off by heart. In the 16th century, it was no problem at all, for schools spent many hours a day teaching Latin to children, so that they could both speak it and write it.

There's no question in my mind that, if you've learned Latin, it helps you with English spelling. It wasn't just the doubling principle that was affected. Many of the spelling decisions that have been made about how to handle individual words have come about because people were thinking 'how was it in Latin?' We'll see the consequences of this mindset in Chapter 21.

Spelling as reputation

'I am the bird of wisdom,' says the owl; 'I was the companion of Pallas Minerva: I am frequently represented in the Egyptian monuments.'

'I have seen you over the British barn-doors,' said the fox, with a grin. 'You have a deal of scholarship, Mrs. Owl. I know a thing or two myself; but am, I confess it, no scholar – a mere man of the world – a fellow that lives by his wits – a mere country gentleman.'

'You sneer at scholarship,' continues the owl, with a sneer on her venerable face. 'I read a good deal of a night.'

'When I am engaged deciphering the cocks and hens at roost,' says the fox.

'It's a pity for all that you can't read; that board nailed over my head would give you some information.'

'What does it say?' says the fox.

'I can't spell in the daylight,' answered the owl; and, giving a yawn, went back to sleep till evening in the hollow of her tree.

(William Makepeace Thackeray, *The Newcombes*, 1855, Ch. 1)

MRS CHEVELEY: Do you know, I am quite looking forward to meeting your clever husband, Lady Chiltern. Since he has been at the Foreign Office, he has been so much talked of in Vienna. They actually succeed in spelling his name right in the newspapers. That in itself is fame, on the continent.

(Oscar Wilde, *An Ideal Husband*, 1895, Act 1)

11
New letters for old

The French scribes eliminated alien-looking Anglo-Saxon letters and replaced them with spellings they found more familiar. The decisions they made introduced some fresh complications into English orthography.

The spelling system at the beginning of the 11th century, the end of the Anglo-Saxon era, was erratic, but no one would describe it as chaotic. It had weaknesses, as we saw in Chapter 5, but it was serviceable. Many of the earlier spelling variations had begun to disappear, as the variety known as West Saxon became more widely used. Yet within 400 years the situation dramatically changed. In 1569, the Chester Herald, John Hart, wrote in *An Orthographie* that English spelling was in a state of 'confusion and disorder'. A few years later, William Bullokar takes up the point, waxing poetical in the Prologue to his own proposal for spelling reform, *The Amendment of Orthographie* (1580):

> *Of which default, complain we may, in the old ABC:*
> *Wherein be letters twenty four, whereof but five agree,*
> *In perfect use, of name and sound, besides misplacing*
>   *some,*

Other are written unsounded, wherein concord is none.

The situation was so bad, he felt, that the only solution was drastic reform: increase the number of letters from twenty-four to forty-four, to make a sort of phonetic alphabet. His system never caught on, but the fact that he devised it at all illustrates the serious nature of his concern. What had happened, to cause such disquiet?

The root cause, as already suggested at the beginning of Chapter 8, was the arrival of the Normans. Although the number of French who took up permanent residence in England after the 1066 invasion was only a few thousand, they held all the important positions in society, accompanied by a cadre of French scribes who took on the tasks of writing official documents, copying manuscripts and compiling the records that would provide the archive of the new nation. Domesday Book was one of their first projects. These scribes brought with them a set of continental spelling habits and expectations, honed through writing Latin and French, that immediately clashed with what they encountered in England. They looked at the way English was being written and didn't like what they saw.

For a start, it looked alien. There were unfamiliar letters in the shape of ash (æ), thorn (þ), eth (ð) and wynn (ƿ), and the g was being written in a curious way, ȝ – a letter that had been borrowed from the Irish alphabet, and which had come to be called 'yogh'. They had to go. As we have seen in earlier chapters, wynn was soon replaced by *w*, and thorn and eth by *th*. We find new spellings: *wall, with, work, write; that, there, think, throw*. Thorn continued in use longer than the others – we find examples as late as the 15th century – and is still reflected, in a curious way, in such usages as 'Ye Olde Tea Shoppe'. *Ye* is a misinterpretation of *þe* 'the'. As thorn fell out of use, people who came across it thought it was a letter Y, which it closely resembled (especially in a black-letter script, *ƿ*). They then pronounced it as a Y – and we continue to do so today, saying 'Yee' Olde Tea Shoppe.

Ash (*æ*) went out of use during the 13th century. The short version of the sound was usually replaced by *a* – so that Old English *Ælfred* became *Alfred*. The long version was replaced by *a, ee* or *e* – so *sæ, sæd* and *æfen* became *sea, seed* and *even*. However, it's important to note that the *æ* spelling we often see today in words like *Cæsar* and *encyclopædia* has a different origin. This was another influence of Latin in the 16th century (as reported in Chapter 11). If *æ* appeared in a Latin word, people felt it should also appear in an English one, and spellings such as *archæologist* and *ætiology* were the result. (The *æ* didn't appeal to Noah Webster, though, who replaced it with an *e* in American English (Chapter 26) – a practice which has been increasingly seen in other varieties of the language over the past hundred years. We now often see in Britain such spellings as *encyclopedia* and *eon*.) Words like *ægis* and *Æsop* kept the two constituent letters but separated them. Most people now write such things as 'under the aegis of the Football Association' and '*Aesop's Fables*'.

The French scribes also had to sort out what to do with the letter yogh (ȝ), which (as we saw in Chapter 5) was being used to write down as many as four consonant sounds. They already had a letter *g*, so they used that to spell the sound /g/, as in *go*. They also used it for the sound /dʒ/, as in *hedge*, spelled *gg* to begin with, and eventually *dg*. The third use of ȝ, to spell the initial sound of words like *ȝear* 'year', wasn't a problem. As the modern spelling shows, they simply used letter *y* for it – hence *yet*, *yield*, *yonder* and *yule*. The fourth use of ȝ – to write the friction consonant that the Anglo-Saxons had used in words like *fuȝol* and *draȝan* – wasn't a problem either, as that sound had disappeared in English speech. Sometime in the early Middle Ages it had weakened and turned into a vowel sound with a 'u' quality. When the French scribes heard this new sound, they spelled it with the similar-sounding *w*: *fuȝol* became *fowl* and *draȝan* became *draw*. And so, by 1500, ȝ had largely disappeared from the writing system. As there was no motivation for the new printing-houses in England to use it – they had no such symbol in the sets of type that they had brought to London from the Continent – the letter simply died out.

In Scotland, the yogh-effect stayed for longer, and there was a slightly different outcome. One problem with yogh had always been its graphic similarity to a *z* written with a long tail. Word-lists would group together words beginning with *ʒ* and those beginning with *z*. Inevitably, people got confused, and as *ʒ* died out, words containing it would automatically be written with a *z*. For example, the word for the wood-grouse, *capercailye*, originally spelled *capercailʒie* in Scotland, came to be spelled *capercailzie* there – though retaining its pronunciation, 'kap-er-kale-yee'. So here we have a very unusual situation: letter *z* being pronounced like a *y*. It couldn't last. Words which had the z-for-yogh spelling eventually attracted the normal pronunciation of *z* – much to the disgust of those who felt that a piece of Scots identity was being lost in the process. Surnames were especially contentious. The *Oxford English Dictionary* has an 18th-century quotation from the Scottish philosopher Lord Kames, who felt that 'pronouncing the letter z in the names Mackenzie and Menzies in the English was enough to turn his stomach'. Names of course do strange things to spelling, as we shall see (Chapter 31). Today, there are still many who insist on the older pronunciation of such names as *Menzies* /mɪŋɪs/ and *Dalziel* /dɪjɛl/. That's why the British politician Menzies Campbell is called 'Ming' for short. But pronouncing 'Mackenzie' in the old style (as 'ma-king-ee') is rare.

Yogh turned up in another context too, and this caused a much more important set of complications in English spelling. In Old English, as we saw in Chapter 5, the letter *h* had been used to spell both the initial /h/ sound in words like *ham* ('home') and the /x/ sound in words like *niht* ('night') and *burh* ('city'). Retaining the letter *h* for the /h/ sound made good sense to scribes familiar with Latin and French, but what to do with the unfamiliar /x/? During the early Middle English period, some scribes had begun to write it with a yogh, so we find such spellings as *niȝt* and *burȝ*. But most scribes, judging by the frequency of spellings, wanted to get away from it. What could they put in its place? They couldn't use *g*, which was already in use, nor *h*, for the same reason. So they opted for a compromise: *gh*. And from the late 1300s we begin to find such spellings as *night* and *burgh* (modern *borough*).

To begin with, that *gh* was pronounced, its actual phonetic quality varying depending on the vowel next to it. But it was a pronunciation that was dying out (though not in Scotland, as we still hear today, and see in such spellings as *nicht* for 'night'). We might have expected the *gh* spellings to disappear along with the sound, but by the time the pronunciation change was widespread the earlier spellings had become thoroughly established. In particular, the printers had opted for it. The very first book printed by William Caxton, in 1471, *The Recuyell* ['compilation'] *of the Historyes of Troy*, has a preface dedicated to Philip Duke of Burgundy, who is described as a 'ryght noble, gloryous and myghty prince'. And increasingly we find instances of 'silent' *gh* – in *right, might, daughter, through* and so on. More on this in Chapter 23.

But not all instances of *gh* became silent. In several words, the letters came to be pronounced as /f/, as in present-day *enough*, *laugh*, *tough*, *chough* and *cough*, and such place names as *'Brough'*. Why /f/? There's a hint of the reason in some of the spellings. Some of the medieval spellings of *laugh*, for example, show an *au* or *aw* before the *gh*, such as *lawghe*. *Enough* has such spellings as *ynowh* and *enohw*. This suggests that the vowel was being pronounced with rounded lips. If we pronounce /u/ and then /f/, we'll notice that both sounds are made with the lips: /u/ has the two lips rounding and coming close together; /f/ has the bottom lip touching the top teeth. It would be a very easy matter to start pronouncing /f/ after a /u/ vowel. (A similar development produced the British pronunciation of *lieutenant*, where the vowel in *lieu* prompted the use of /v/ or /f/ – we find such early spellings as *lievetenant* and *lieftenant* – the latter, influenced by the following /t/, becoming the norm.)

The change happened quite early: there are 15th- and 16th-century spellings such as *laffe* for *laugh*, *enoff* for *enough*, *tuffe* for *tough*, and *choff* for *chough*. The only surprise, we might think, is that not more words were affected. But actually several other words did do the same thing, though they later dropped the /f/, such as *daughter* (as indicated by old spellings such as *doffter*) and *dough* (the /f/ still remembered in the modern word *plum duff*, i.e. plum dough). And if we look at all regional dialects, we'll find many more examples. Joseph Wright, in his *English Dialect*

Dictionary (1898–1905), records many dialect pronunciations of *gh* words in which the /f/ is present, all from parts of the north of England. *Plough*, for example, turns up as *plawf, pleaf, pleaff, pleeaf, pleuf, plewf, plif, pliff, pluf, plufe, pluff* and *pluif*. An /f/ ending can sometimes still be heard today.

While the French scribes were working out what to do with the consonant letters, they had to cope with a different kind of problem: how to represent a pronunciation of English consonants that was steadily changing.

12
Old letters in new words

Several Old English words had their spellings changed by the French scribes, even though they contained letters that were used in French. Some new spelling patterns were the result.

Once the alien-looking letters had been eliminated, the French scribes wouldn't have expected there to be many other problems. French and English had several sounds in common, after all, and the spellings were the same. And if they found an Anglo-Saxon spelling practice unpalatable, it was going to be a simple matter to replace it with a corresponding French one. The choice between *s* and *c*, in particular, attracted a lot of attention.

We've already seen that the Old English *sc* spelling (in words like *scip*) was replaced by *sh* (Chapter 8), or sometimes *sch*. And evidently the French scribes didn't like the look of words ending in *s* either. Already in Old English there were such spellings as *mys* ('mice'), *lys* ('lice'), *is* ('ice') and *fleos* ('fleece'), and these were hugely increased by an influx of new French words ending in this sound. To begin with, some of them continued to be spelled in an Anglo-Saxon way: French *service*, for example, appeared as *serfise*, *servis* and suchlike. But it didn't last. Today, all are spelled with the French preference, *-ce*: *service, since, dance, fence, truce, price, face, juice* ...

Of course, once a new spelling arrived, it could be exploited, and a good example is the way *-ce* and *-se* were then used to distinguish awkward word pairs. These were cases where the same basic word was used both as a noun and a verb by changing just a single sound. *Advice* was now able to contrast with *advise*, and *device* with *devise*. A similar distinction is seen in *prophecy* and *prophesy*. But it was a short-lived gain. In the 17th century, some spelling authorities decided that the distinction was so useful that it should be extended to two other verb/noun pairs: *practise* and *practice*, *license* and *licence*. They ignored the fact that there was no difference in pronunciation in these cases, and so another complication for modern learners was born. British English eventually retained the distinction, thanks partly to the influence of Dr Johnson's *Dictionary* (Chapter 25), which recognised *practice* and *practise* and included several examples of *licence* as a noun. However, American lexicographer Noah Webster (Chapter 26) found no merit in these last two, which is why in American English we see the *ise* spelling in all four forms.

Occasionally a French word interfered with *s* in other parts of a word too. Many Old English words began with *s*, as in modern *say, send, sell, same, see, sin*, etc. – and *sinder* was one of them, referring to the residue left by metal in a furnace. French had a different word, *cendre*, meaning 'ashes' (as left behind in a fire). Evidently the similarity in meaning caused the two words to be linked, because from the 15th century we find *sinder* spelled with both *c* and *s*, and eventually the *c* became the norm.

Murder also shows the influence of French. This was *morðor* in Old English, and it became *morthor* when the letter eth was replaced by *th* in Middle English (Chapter 11). Various spellings are found, but there's a *th* in all of them to begin with. Then gradually we see the effect of the ways this word was spelled in French, such as *mortre* and *murdre*. The *o* becomes a *u*, though there was probably hardly any change in the pronunciation, and the *th* is spelled with a *d*. But the 'th' pronunciation stayed for a long time. It was still there in Shakespeare's day, and indeed it will still be heard today in some regional dialects, such as Irish English.

Rich was another Old English word which went in an unexpected direction. We might have expected it to be spelled *ritch*, like *witch*, *itch* and many others, and indeed such spellings as *ritch* and *rytche* are attested in Middle English. But there are several spellings with a *ch* too, such as *rych* and *riche*. It's likely that writers were being influenced by the French word, *riche*, and eventually it was the French spelling that won.

The 'appeal' of French spelling shouldn't surprise

us, for we see the same thing happening today. It would have been perfectly possible to spell the name of the small, trendy shops and hotels that began to appear in the 1950s as *bouteeks*, but the connotations of the spelling *boutiques* evidently had greater appeal. Several French words ending in -*que* convey the same fashionable associations, such as *critique*, *plaque*, *marque*, *baroque*, *humoresque* and *discotheque*. All of them might have been respelled to end in *k* or *ck*, with no change in pronunciation. Indeed, in a few cases, alternative spellings did develop, notably between British *cheque* and *chequers* vs. American *check* and *checkers*. Similar variations can be found in earlier centuries too, such as *mask* and *masque*, though in this case different meanings evolved.

In cases like *service* and *cinder*, we have a fairly straightforward situation: the sounds stay the same, the spellings change. But the French scribes also had to cope with a much trickier state of affairs. Old sounds were being used in new ways.

Tarzan learns to read

Among the other books were a primer, some child's readers, numerous picture books, and a great dictionary. All of these he examined, but the pictures caught his fancy most, though the strange little bugs which covered the pages where there were no pictures excited his wonder and deepest thought.

His little face was tense in study, for he had partially grasped, in a hazy, nebulous way, the rudiments of a thought which was destined to prove the key and the solution to the puzzling problem of the strange little bugs …

In his hands was a primer opened at a picture of a little ape similar to himself, but covered, except for hands and face, with strange, colored fur, for such he thought the jacket and trousers to be. Beneath the picture were three little bugs –

Boy.

And now he had discovered in the text upon the page that these three were repeated many times in the same sequence.

Another fact he learned – that there were comparatively few individual bugs; but these were repeated many times, occasionally alone, but more often in company with others.

Slowly he turned the pages, scanning the pictures and the text for a repetition of the combination B-O-Y. Presently he found it beneath a picture of another little ape and a strange animal which went upon four legs like the jackal and resembled him not a little. Beneath this picture the bugs appeared as:

A Boy and a Dog

There they were, the three little bugs which always accompanied the little ape.

And so he progressed very, very slowly, for it was a hard and laborious task which he had set himself without knowing it – a task which might seem to you or me impossible – learning to read without having the slightest knowledge of letters or written language, or the faintest idea that such things existed.

He did not accomplish it in a day, or in a week, or in a month, or in a year; but slowly, very slowly, he learned after he had grasped the possibilities which lay in those little bugs, so that by the time he was fifteen he knew the various combinations of letters which stood for every pictured figure in the little primer and in one or two of the picture books.

(From Edgar Rice Burroughs, *Tarzan of the Apes*, 1914, Ch. 7)

Actor Gordon Scott as Tarzan in 1958

13

Old sounds in new positions

Sometimes an Old English sound began to be used in a new position within a word. The old spelling would not always work well in the new position, and a fresh solution had to be found.

A sound can turn up in a word in three positions: at the beginning, in the middle, or at the end. Some sounds appear in all three: /p/, for example, is heard in *pie, taper* and *rip*. Some sounds don't appear at the beginning: the /ŋ/ sound, spelled *ng*, is rare at the beginning of a word in English; an /h/ sound, spelled *h*, is never heard at the end. Several consonant and vowel sounds have restrictions governing where in a word they can be used.

Quite often, in the history of a language, a sound that is usually heard in one position begins to be used in another. When this happens, there are immediate implications for the spelling. Can the spelling transfer along with the sound? This question had to be faced in the early Middle Ages, as a result of the impact of French on English, with the /dʒ/ consonant we hear at the end of words like *hedge*. In Old

English, this sound was only ever used after a vowel. But in the Middle English period, words began to arrive from French beginning with this sound, such as *gentle*, *gem*, *joy* and *jewel*. How were they to be spelled?

Several of the French words were spelled with a *g*, so that was one possibility – but *g* in English was already strongly associated with the plosive sound in words such as *go*. An alternative was to use a *y*, already being used in such words as *year* and *yet*, as we saw in Chapter 11 – but that could be confusing, suggesting that *joy*, for instance, should be pronounced as 'yoy'. A third possibility was to use letter *i*, which was sometimes found representing a consonant at the beginning of a word; but that would mean this letter would represent both a consonant sound and a vowel sound – something scribes liked to avoid if at all possible. And the fourth was to use letter *j*, which was beginning to appear as a separate letter shape in English. That looked like a much more promising solution.

J was originally a variant form of *i*, introduced to help the reader when there was a sequence of two or more *i* letters. How to make Roman numerals such as *ii*, *iii* and *viii* easier to read? Simply add a tail to the final *i* and write them *ij*, *iij* and *viij*. Anglo-Saxon scribes had little need of such a convention in Old English, apart from writing some Latin words, such as *filij* ('son'). It was never thought of as a letter in its own right; it was simply a 'long' *i*. But several

European languages were beginning to exploit it as a way of showing a consonant sound.

The French scribes explored all four of the options. At various times we see *gentle* spelled *gentil, iantyl, jantil* and *yentyll*, among a host of other variants. Versions of *joy* include *ioie, goye, yoye* and *joye*. Versions of *jewel* include *yewel, gewel, iewel* and *jewel*. Eventually the *j* forms predominated, as we now know, being used before all the main vowel letters – *jazz, jest, jig, job, jump*. But the use of *g* for the same sound was kept in a number of cases where there is a following letter *e* or *i*, as in *gentle, germ, gibber* and *ginger*.

Thanks to the vacillation, which continued for several hundred years, we have a problem today. A *g* followed by an *e* or *i* can be interpreted in either of two ways: as representing a /g/ or a /dʒ/ sound. Later words entering the language sometimes went one way, sometimes the other. On the one hand we have *gentle, gem* and *geography*; on the other we have *get, gear* and *geyser*. *Ginger* exists alongside *gingham*; *gigantic* along with *giggle*; *gibber* with *gibbon*; *gemstone* with *gemsbok*. A third sound is sometimes heard: /ʒ/, as in the initial letter of *gigue* and *gigolo*. Sometimes the uncertainty about how to interpret the letter has led to alternative pronunciations, especially in technical words such as *gelada, gerbera* and *gimbals*, and many people are uncertain about how to say such words as *genus* and *gerontology*. I still have no idea how best to say *geegaw*!

Spelling as stratagem

He (*who has failed to catch his companion's name, and wishes to find it out indirectly*).
"By the way, how do you *spell* your name?"
She. "J-O-N-E-S."

(From *Mr Punch in Society*, c. 1900, p. 91)

14
New sounds in old places

Some of the spoken consonants from Old English began to be used in new ways, to distinguish words. The French scribes had to adapt their system to show that these words differed in meaning.

Another big feature of the developing sound system of Middle English arose from the way speakers were beginning to use old sounds to distinguish new words. In Old English, the sounds /f/ and /v/ both existed, but they weren't used to distinguish words. *Wif* ('wife') ended in an /f/; but when this sound appeared between vowels, as in *wifian* ('to take a wife'), it was influenced by the voicing of those vowels and was pronounced like a /v/. The name of *Eve* in the Bible, though pronounced with a /v/, was spelled with an *f – Efa*. There was no pair of words where the only distinction was the switch from /f/ to /v/, as in modern *fan* and *van*.

This changed in the early Middle English period. The French scribes heard the two sounds and spelled them differently: an *f* for the voiceless sound /f/, and a *u* (later *v*) for the voiced sound /v/. It was a familiar contrast to them, for there were word pairs in French that were already being differentiated by /f/ and /v/ – as in that language today, such as *fin*, 'end' and *vin*, 'wine'. They were also well used to seeing words with a *v* spelling in Latin. So gradually we hear the contrast emerging in English between *wife* and *wive*, *knife* and *knive*, and other pairs.

The process was hastened by the arrival of new words from French. Some contrasted with a previously existing English word, such as *view* (French) and *few* (Old English) or *veal* (French) and *feel* (Old English). In other cases, both words were French imports, such as *save* and *safe*. And once the pattern was established, /v/ and /f/ became a regular feature of the sound system, being used to distinguish words from any source. We later find Old English *fast* alongside Latin *vast*, Old English *fear* alongside Dutch *veer*, and other such pairs.

The dialect variation in England would have helped this process: words beginning with /f/ were pronounced with a /v/ in many parts of the south, so that we see *for* spelled *vor*, *father* spelled *vader* and so on. Some of these regional spellings actually became part of the standard language in due course. That's why, for example, we have *vixen* alongside *fox*, and why we have both *vat* and *fat*, *van* and *fan*, *vane* and *fane*. All this would have helped to provide an orthographic climate in which the new French words beginning with *v* would appear less alien. We can see the change taking place in a word like *verse*, which had arrived in Old English from Latin as *fers*. This had carried over into Middle English: Orrm (Chapter 7), for example, spells it as *ferrs*, and that is in the 12th century. But the *f* was very soon replaced by a *v*.

Exactly the same situation applied to the difference between /s/ and /z/. In Old English, as with /f/ and /v/, both sounds existed. *Hus* ('house') ended in an /s/; but when this sound appeared between vowels, as in *husian* ('to provide with a house'), it was influenced by the voicing of those vowels and was pronounced like a /z/. (We hear this effect today still, in *houses* and *housing*.) There was no pair of words where the only distinction was the switch from /s/ to /z/ – as in modern *bus* and *buzz*.

Here, too, things changed in Middle English. French scribes were familiar with the contrast between /s/ and /z/, so when they heard a /z/ sound in an Old English word, they were minded to spell it differently from /s/. One possibility was to use *se*, and some scribes did try this out, but it proved to be ambiguous. *Grase*, for example, was used in early Middle English as a spelling of both *graze* (in its sense of 'eat grass' – *grasian* in Old English) and *grace* (a French arrival in the 12th century). It wasn't a satisfactory solution and eventually the spellings diverged, resulting in the forms we have today.

As more words arrived from French with a /z/ sound, the letter *z* was increasingly used. The Old English word *segel* had evolved into *seal*. Then in 1382, John Wycliffe introduced a French word *zeal* in his translation of the Bible, and he spelled it with a z. Sometimes two French words go in different directions, as in *prize* and *price, seize* and *cease*. But z evidently never had the appeal of other letters. It's even used as an insult in Shakespeare: in *King Lear* (II. 2. 61), Kent insults the steward Oswald by saying 'Thou whoreson zed! thou unnecessary letter.' And so, with z on the wane, we find *se* continuing to be used as an alternative – hence *pease* along with *peace*, and *lose* along with *loose*. In rare instances, they had to distinguish three words, and had to call upon z as well, as in *raze* and *race* (from French), alongside *raise* (from Scandinavia).

Why was z unattractive? We get a hint of the reason in a book published in 1582 by the headmaster of Merchant Taylors' School in London, Richard Mulcaster: *The Elementarie, which entreateth chieflie of the right writing of our English tung* (pp. 96, 123). It was a difficult letter to write quickly. There he says (I modernise the spelling and punctuation) that 'Z is a consonant much heard amongst us and seldom seen. I think by reason it is not so ready to the pen as *s* is, which is become lieutenant general to z.' (A lieutenant general was someone delegated to take command in place of a ruler.) He also feels that z has an alien character: 'It is not lightly [i.e. frequently] expressed in English, saving in foreign enfranchisements [i.e. borrowings].' So he concludes: 'A form that is fair to the eye in print, and cumbersome to the hand in penning, is not to pass in writing.'

Clearly the antagonism to *z* must have been strong among scribes, otherwise such doublets as *close* (the adjective, with /s/) and *to close* (the verb, with /z/) or *house* (the noun, with /s/) and *to house* (the verb, with /z/) would never have survived. A *z* would inevitably have appeared. Indeed, we see exactly that process happening centuries later. When 20th-century psychologists wanted a word to describe a type of test in which readers have to supply omitted words (as in *The house was spick and* —), they used the phonetic spelling, shortening the word *closure*, and called it a *cloze test*.

Uncertainty over whether to use *s* or *z* to spell the /z/ sound continued over the centuries. Until the 16th century, *gaze, amaze* and *razor* were spelled both ways, then *z* prevailed. *Tease, bruise* and *surprise* were spelled both ways until as late as the 19th century, when *s* prevailed. We find several variations in Shakespeare. The First Folio usually spells verbs ending in -*ize* or -*ise* with *z*, as in *sympathize, canonize, memorize* and many more; but we find *advertise, compromise* and *enfranchise* most often spelled with *s*.

If anything has come to popularise the letter *z* in modern times it is the -*ize* ending, as it is a very frequent way of forming new verbs. This spelling was preferred by classical scholars, especially in the 16th century, as they felt it more closely reflected the way the words were spelled in Greek and Latin, and that historical argument has fostered the use of *z* ever since. The USA and Canada adopted it from the outset. James Murray, the first editor of the *Oxford English Dictionary,* also opted for it, at the end of the 19th century, partly on historical grounds and partly on the grounds that this letter better reflects the sound. This influenced Horace Hart, who compiled his *Rules for Compositors and Readers at the University Press, Oxford.* He opens his first booklet with a section on spellings, and adopts the *-ize* spellings used in Murray's dictionary. Murray, in turn, had been influenced by Dr Johnson, whose *Dictionary* has *agonize, analyze, anatomize* and so on (see further, Chapter 25).

So where did the *-ise* alternatives come from? Some of the words (such as *baptize*) were spelled with both an *s* and a *z* from their earliest days in Middle English. The trend to spell all such verbs with *s* began when verbs came into English with increasing frequency from French, where the suffix was *-iser.* A verb of this kind, borrowed directly from French, it was argued, should be spelled with *-ise* to reflect that source. Some felt it important to maintain a spelling link between related words, such as *analyse* and *analyst.* And during the 19th century, this usage grew.

The problem, of course, is that it is often unclear whether a verb has come into English from French (so, use *s*) or from Latin (so, use *z*). Confusion led 19th-century printers to try to sort it out, and they did this by imposing a uniform rule for all such verbs where alternatives exist. Hart, as we've seen, opted for *-ize*. But several other publishers – perhaps in an effort to distinguish themselves from Oxford – opted for *-ise*. They may also have been influenced by the fact that there are fewer exceptions if you go for the *-ise* rule. Several verbs can only appear in *-ise*, and you have to remember what they are:

> advertise, advise, apprise, chastise, circumcise, comprise, compromise, despise, devise, excise, exercise, franchise, improvise, incise, revise, supervise, surmise, surprise, televise

This isn't a complete list, because there are derived forms (such as *enfranchise, misadvise*) as well as new usages (*to merchandise, an enterprising proposal*) to take into account. Also, uncertainty over what the 'rule' is means that we sometimes see some of these verbs spelled with a *z*, especially in the USA.

World usage varies: *-ize* is the overall preference in North America; *-ise* in Australia. Usage in the UK is mixed, with *-ise* beating *-ize* in a ratio of 3:2. But practice is changing, with American usage steadily encroaching on British (Chapter 26). Some publishers these days are adopting a more relaxed attitude: they don't mind which authors use, as long as they are consistent. Personally, having had my usage pushed first one way and then the other by publishers over the years, I've given up having a preference.

The same change that affected *f* / *v* and *s* / *z* also applied to the two *th* pronunciations of Old English (Chapter 11). Today these sounds can differentiate words, as heard in modern *thigh* vs. *thy*

or *wreath* vs. *wreathe*. But unlike the other new con-
trasts, the spelling stayed the same for both sounds.
The reason is probably that not many words were
affected. French didn't have the *th* sound, so no new
instances of its use would come from that direction.
And there are very few examples like *thigh* and *thy*.
Most of the words where you have to know that *th*
is pronounced as /ð/ not /θ/ belong to a very small
set, chiefly *the, this, that, these, those, there, their, then,*
than, thou, thee, thy, thine, they, them and *though*. They
are high frequency words that are more to do with
grammar than vocabulary. In the case of *with*, we can
use either pronunciation. It's easy to see why the
scribes felt there was no need for a new spelling convention to handle such a small set of special cases.
People would quickly learn them as exceptions.

But these exceptions weren't the only ones.

15
More exceptions

The style of handwriting used by the medieval scribes caused certain sequences of letters to look identical. Various solutions were found to distinguish the words, but in many cases new irregular spellings were the outcome.

Several words in English spelling have been influenced by the cursive handwriting style used by medieval scribes. *Cursive* comes from Latin *currere* 'to run', and refers to a way of writing the letters in a word in which the pen doesn't leave the page. Today we'd say the letters were 'run together', or 'joined up'. But, as we all know from our own experience, joined-up writing can be much more difficult to read than a style where the letters are kept separate (as when we write something out in capital letters).

The scribes – not just in England, but all over Europe – soon noticed that one feature of the cursive style was causing especial problems. Several letters were formed by a short downstroke of the pen, called a *minim* (from Latin *minimus* 'smallest'). An *i* (without a dot) was a single minim. An *n, u* or *v* would be two minims. An *m* or *w* would be three. And when these letters were adjacent in a word, there were unexpected difficulties of interpretation. Take a word like *mine*, spelled in early Middle English as *min*. If I show a minim by a downstroke |, then *min* would come out as ||||||. How might this sequence of six minims be read? It could be interpreted as any combination of the relevant letters – *win*, *nim* ('take'), *nun* ... A word written as *t*||||*e* could be read as *time*, *twie* ('twice') or *tune*. If somebody actually wrote down the word *minim* in that style, it would be *ten* undifferentiated strokes. Context would help to decode what was intended, in some cases, but there would be a lot of guesswork on the part of the reader. Easy reading it wasn't.

Several new orthographic practices were devised to help. One of the earliest was the simple expedient of distinguishing letter *i* by adding a dot on top of the minim. The practice started in Latin manuscripts during the 11th century. At first, only the *i* next to other minims was dotted, but eventually all occurrences of the letter were written in that way. Some scribes added other distinguishing features to *i*, such as giving it an extra flourish or adding a tail (a practice which led to the letter *j*, as we saw in Chapter 13). But in print, the simple dot sufficed, and this ultimately influenced all forms of handwriting.

The other strategy to distinguish *i* was to replace it with *y*. The two letters had come to represent similar sounds, because the rounded sound of a *y* in

Old English (Chapter 5) had been lost. So, if *i* was difficult to read, use a *y* instead. We find *myn* being used as well as *min* ('mine'), *tyme* as well as *time* and so on. The most interesting development was the way scribes took against using the letter *i* as the final letter in a word. They preferred to write *body* for *bodi*, *holy* for *holi*, *ready* for *readi*. It didn't seem to worry them when such words needed an ending such as a plural, so that the *i* wasn't final, as they retained the *i* there. That's why we spell the plural of *body* as *bodies*, not *bodyes*, and have such forms as *holier* (not *holyer*), *carries* (not *carryes*) and *worrisome* (not *worrysome*). This alternation has become a basic spelling 'rule' today.

The similarity of sound between *y* and *ie* led to a long period when the two spellings were interchangeable. In Middle English we find both *fly* and *flie*, *ready* and *readie*. Two hundred years later, in Shakespeare texts, we still see *bodie* and *body*, *canopie* and *canopy*, *carrie* and *carry*, *carryed* and *carried*. But by the 18th century, the modern forms had been largely established. Letter *y* wins in final position, and in certain other locations – before an *-ing* ending to avoid an *ii* sequence (so we spell *flying* not *fliing*) and before a plural ending if a vowel precedes (so we spell *boys* not *boies* – three vowel letters together has never appealed to English writers). Today, we see a final *i* only in later foreign loanwords and names, such as *rabbi*, *Magi*, *khaki*, *ski*, *origami* and *tsunami*, and in the plurals of words borrowed from Italian or

Latin, such as *spaghetti, graffiti* and *stimuli*. There are
still a few loose ends: is it *aunty* or *auntie*? *nighty* or
nightie? *calory* or *calorie*? Is the name *Fanny* or *Fannie*?

The legacy of the overlap between *i* and *y* is still
with us, though, and causes a great deal of present-
day pain. We have both *dye* ('colour') and *die* ('lose
life'), and thus *dyeing* and *dying* (never *dieing* – the
three-vowel avoidance again). But how many of
us could ever honestly say we haven't sometimes
paused over which is which? We only have to type
'dying hair' into Google to see the millions who omit
the *e*. The situation isn't helped by the usage variants
which have developed. So, we have *tyres, gypsies* and
cyphers in British English, but *tires, gipsies* and *ciphers*
in American, with US usage increasingly influencing
traditional British. And is it a *flyer* or a *flier* (in any of
its senses)? Here usage has varied for centuries, both
within and between English-speaking countries.

But what about the other minims? Was there anything that could be done to help readers work out
how to read sequences where a *u* was followed by a
v, n or *m*? Several words fell into this category, such
as *cum* ('come'), *sum* ('some'), *huni* ('honey'), *tung*
('tongue') and *luv* ('love'). These would all appear
as a consonant followed by four or five minims.
Munuc ('monk') would be a sequence of nine. The
problem remained even if these words were spelled
with a final *e*. So, as the modern spellings immediately show, they hit on the idea of replacing the *u*
with an *o*. We see them especially after a *w* – *worry*,

worse, worm, wonder, won, wolf, wort, woman ... Not all such changes were permanent. *Plunge*, for example, began life as *plunge* (from French *plunger*), switched to *plonge*, and then went back to *plunge* – probably another instance of French influence (Chapter 12).

The strategy had some immediate benefits. It meant, for example, that *son* would no longer be confused with *sun*. But, as always with spelling reform, there was a downside. Look at what happened to *tongue*. By rights, this should today be spelled *tung*, as with *rung, sung, lung, hung* and suchlike. But anyone who began to spell *tung* as *tong* in the 14th century would soon encounter a different sort of clash: with *tongs* (the lifting implement). Both words often appeared with a final *e*: *tonge*. But a final -*ge* spelling, as we saw in Chapter 5, was being pronounced /dʒ/, as in *refuge, visage* and so on. So, *tonge* would look as if it was to be pronounced to rhyme with *sponge*. Several scribes must have wondered: 'How do we get out of this one?' They had to show that the final *g* was hard, a /g/. Some tried *tounghe*. But *tongue* won. And eventually, in some accents (such as Received Pronunciation), speakers dropped the /g/ sound, so that the wheel came full circle: *tongue* for them now does indeed rhyme with *lung*. It's regular in sound, but highly irregular in spelling. (*Tongs* simply dropped the *e*, and now rhymes nicely with *wrongs*.)

The minim argument has its limitations. If it were as big an issue as is suggested above, then we'd expect more words to have changed; but we still see *u* next to *m* or *n* surviving in many words with the same vowel sound, /ʌ/, such as *thumb, hunt* and *under*. We must also be careful not to extend the minim explanation to words with the same vowel sound where there was already an *o* in the spelling, such as *among* (from Old English) and *money* (from French *monai*). An *o* was also being used in similar-sounding words where there were no minims, such as *borough, thorough* and *worry*.

The fact is that there are very few word pairs like *win* and *nun* which would be confused, and it's difficult to see how there would ever have been real ambiguity. People don't read words in isolation, or letter-by-letter – they rely on context. The minims in a sentence like *She became a* ||||| are never going to be misread as *win*. Those in *I shall* ||||| *the race* are never going to be misread as *nun*. Concern over minims undoubtedly accounted for some changes in the spelling of words containing sequences of *w, u, i, m* and *n*, but not all.

The situation was becoming very complex. During the Middle English period, new French spellings had been grafted onto old Anglo-Saxon practices by a cadre of scribes who must at times have felt quite out of their depth. They had come up with all sorts of decisions to make the conflation work, and then had to cope with some of the unforeseen consequences of those decisions. Few at the outset had any training in English, either as a language or as a writing system. Unfamiliar with English dialect differences, they would not have appreciated the spelling variations that reflected different regional pronunciations. They were working as individuals or in small groups. There was no national planning, no coordination other than occasional points of contact between individual scribal centres. And so we find a huge amount of variation in spellings during the Middle English period. A word like *night*, for example, was being spelled in dozens of different ways. The *Oxford English Dictionary* records over sixty variants at that time (shown here in alphabetical order):

> neght, neghte, neyʒt, neyʒte, neyʒth, neyth, nhyht, nichʒ, nicht, nichte, nicst, nict, nieht, nig, night, nighte, nigt, nih, nihht, niht, niʒht, nihte, nihtt, nijʒt, nikte, nist, niʒst, niʒt, niʒte, niʒth, niʒtt, nite, nith, nithe, niþt, noyʒth, nycht, nygh, nyght, nyghte, nyghth, nyghtt, nygt, nygth, nygthe, nygtt, nyhet, nyht, nyhte, nyhyt, nyt, nyte, nyth, nythe, nytʒ, nyught, nyʒ, nyʒht, nyʒt, nyʒte, nyʒth, nyʒthe, nyʒtht, nyʒtt

The variation wouldn't have bothered 13th-century scribes. In the absence of any clear notion of 'correct spelling', they had a mindset which was very different to what we have today. To spell a word differently in a single manuscript, or even within a single line, was simply not an issue.

Is it possible to say why a scribe might opt for one spelling rather than another? We can't identify individuals, of course, apart from a few rare instances where the scribes are known, but we can certainly get a sense of the factors that would have been most influential. Sometimes a completely irrelevant factor intervened – irrelevant, that is, from a linguistic point of view. For example, lawyers' clerks were paid for their writing by the inch, so longer words meant more money for them (much as, I suppose, when journalists are paid by the word today). One would earn nearly twice as much if *musik* was spelled *musiycque* or *had* was spelled *hadde*. In the 16th century, Richard Mulcaster looked disapprovingly at the practice in his *Elementarie* (p. 86): 'If words be overcharged with number of letters, that comes either by covetousness in such as sell them by lines, or by ignorance.' It was one of the practices he worked hard to eliminate – and with some success.

There were also linguistic factors at work influencing a scribe's preferences for a particular spelling. Two of them are especially interesting because they show the way scribes were being pulled in contradictory directions. We look at these in the next two chapters.

Avoiding the vulgar

The dog sleeps on my bed, and I had a bad night with him, he disturbed me so, and I am afraid I am very stupid this morning. His name is Tommie. We are obliged to call him by it, because he won't answer to any other than the name he had when my Lady bought him. But we spell it with an *ie* at the end, which makes it less vulgar than Tommy with a *y*.

(Wilkie Collins, *My Lady's Money: An Episode in the Life of a Young Girl*, 1879, Ch. 4)

16

Showing the difference

Quite a few words in English sound the same but differ in meaning, or look the same but differ in sound. The differences are sometimes shown in the spelling and sometimes not.

As the examples in the last few chapters illustrate, the French scribes did more than simply introduce French spelling conventions wherever they could. They adapted them to suit the lexicon of the new language. It was a language with a very different structure from French. French was a language which relied on word-endings and gender for its grammatical relationships; and while English grammar had earlier used these features, most of them had been lost by the beginning of the Middle English period. Additionally, as we've seen, some vowels had changed their pronunciation. The result was that several words which might once have been distinguished by different endings now sounded the same.

What should be done in these cases? The scribes might have left them all with the same spelling. If the sound /juː/ could refer to a kind of tree, a female sheep and a second-person pronoun, it was unlikely that they would ever be confused. They might all have been spelled *you*, therefore, so that today we would read about a *you-tree* or *a ram and a you*. But it seems the scribes didn't think like that. Rather, if words had different functions – different meanings, or different grammatical uses (such as noun and verb) – then they felt they should be spelled differently. And although there was a great deal of variation to begin with, eventually these words ended up as *yew, ewe* and *you*. There are around 500 examples remaining like this in Modern English. Most are just pairs of words, like *bear* and *bare*, but we can find as many as four coming together with the same pronunciation, as in *pause, pours, pores* and *paws* – though whether the pronunciations are exactly the same depends on the speaker's accent. When they are identical, we call them *homophones* – words that sound the same but differ in meaning.

It's easy to see how homophones can develop different spellings. In Old English we find the first use of the word which in Modern English is spelled *peak*. In the 14th century along comes a similar-sounding word, and today we spell it as *peek*. In the 16th century we find another arrival which today is spelled *pique*. And in the 20th century, a fourth word arrives, an abbreviation for a type of dog, a *peke*. They might all have been spelled in the same way, but it's clear that writers felt the need to keep them separate.

Other examples? English has maintained a

spelling difference between *right, rite, wright* and *write; carrot, carat* and *caret; sight, site* and *cite; altar* and *alter; cereal* and *serial; tale* and *tail;* and *sow* and *sew.* A major difference in meaning seems to have motivated a different spelling. We can sense a similar pressure on us today, when a new word arrives and we have to decide how to spell it. When *mousse* came into English in the 19th century, people accepted its French spelling to distinguish it from *moose.* The motor industry's *marque* distinguished it from *mark.* And today the search for fresh spellings is part of everyday commercial life (Chapter 30).

Nonetheless, this is not a dominant feature of English spelling. Five hundred homophonous pairs might seem a lot, but it is not five thousand or fifty thousand. The vast majority of words in English which have the same sound but different uses have the same spelling, such as *present* (the gift) and *present* (the time). The noun *charge* can refer to explosives, electricity, accusation, attacking, payment and much more. We spell *round* in the same way regardless of its part of speech: as noun (*a round*), verb (*to round*), adjective (*round shape*), preposition (*round the corner*) and adverb (*come round*).

It's not difficult to see why this should be the case. Most words in everyday English have more than one meaning. If each of these meanings had to have a different spelling, the complexity of the spelling system would be hugely increased. And where would we stop? Would a figurative use of a word have to have a different spelling from its literal use, so that *cold weather*, for example, would have to be spelled differently from a *cold face*? No spelling system could possibly cope with this.

So why are there any homophonic spelling differences in English at all? Etymology is the chief reason: if scribes were aware that two homophones had different origins and different spelling histories – as with *right, rite, wright* and *write* – then they saw them as very distinct entities and maintained a spelling difference. They must also have been sensitive to the possibility that some of these homophones could cause real confusion. And when we think of the way homophones are used in jokes, riddles, puns, poetry and other kinds of ludic activity, we can see how this might be. We'll find dozens of examples in any modern collection of 'jokes for kids', such as this (mercifully short) selection:

> Have you heard the story about the skyscraper? It's a tall story/storey.
> Have you heard the story about the peacock? It's a beautiful tale/tail.
> If f means forte, what does ff mean? Eighty.
> Why do we call money bread? Because everybody kneads/needs it.
> Why did the chicken cross the road? For fowl/foul purposes.

This kind of punning is by no means restricted to children. Once we have learned how to do it, it stays with us for the rest of our lives, as when adults pun on *prophet* and *profit* or *jeans* and *genes*. Authors frequently pun in this way. The opening lines of Shakespeare's *Richard III* provide a famous example:

> *Now is the winter of our discontent*
> *Made glorious summer by this sun of York ...*

The play is on *sun* and *son*, for Richard is a son of the Duke of York. There are thousands of examples like this in Shakespeare. But if a literary author can exploit a homophonous pair to make a point, then in everyday speech the same contrast can be a source of ambiguity. It's easy to see how scribes might strive to maintain a spelling difference under such circumstances.

The same question arises in relation to *homographs*: words with different meaning which have the same spelling but differ in pronunciation. Why do these exist at all? We see them in *row* (a boat) and *row* (a quarrel), *tear* (from the eye) and *tear* (rip), *wind* (breeze) and *wind* (turn), *bow* (weapon) and *bow* (the head). There aren't many of these – a few dozen, rather than a few hundred – but why have any? Surely, over the centuries, these words should have ended up being spelled differently?

The answer has to be that the differences of grammar and meaning between such pairs were so great that they never actually caused anyone a reading problem. Nobody would ever read the sentence *I'm going to tear it up*, and think it referred to crying, or *A tear fell from her eye* and think it was

something to do with ripping. Context is everything in such cases. The only surprise is that a few
of these homographic word pairs stayed unchanged
on the rare occasions when context was no help. For
example, there are times when it's difficult to decide
whether *read* is present tense or past, as in this fragment of dialogue:

> Are you aware of what's going on in the bank?
> Yes, I read about it in the papers.

And does *learned* in *a learned response* mean 'instructed'
or 'highly educated'? Why didn't such spellings as
redd and *learnedd* evolve? Presumably ambiguous
instances like these were so infrequent that people
felt they could live with them – as for the most part
we do today. Just occasionally we sense a discomfort, as when writers try to get their meaning across
by doing something very un-English: using a grave
accent – *learnèd*.

There may not be very many homophones and
homographs in English, but some of the words
which illustrate them are of frequent occurrence –
such as *no* and *know*, *here* and *hear*, *too* and *two* – so
the problem is always in front of our eyes. On the
other hand, the fact that they are frequent means that
learners get lots of practice in reading and writing
them, so they are less of a problem than we might
think. We must also remember that the learning of
such pairs usually takes place over a period of time,
so that children get used to one spelling before they

encounter the other – *boy* a long time before *buoy*, for example, or *story* before *storey*.

The time factor is very important. A big mistake, in teaching children to spell, is to present them with pairs of homophones or homographs at the same time. It's even worse when they are presented in isolation (see Appendix I). I have children's books on my shelf whose authors think they are being helpful by presenting pairs of items on opposite pages – a little boy with a watch on one side and looking at tiny insects on the other. The pictures are fun, but all we see linguistically is *minute* and *minute*. This doesn't help.

Charles Dickens and his characters reflect upon spelling

He'll never read. He can make all the letters separately, and he knows most of them separately when he sees them; he has got on that much, under me; but he can't put them together. He's too old to acquire the knack of it now – and too drunk.

(Tony Jobling, of Mr Krook, in *Bleak House*, 1852–3, Ch. 32)

'What's your name, sir?' inquired the judge.

'Sam Weller, my lord,' replied that gentleman.

'Do you spell it with a "V" or a "W"?' inquired the judge.

'That depends upon the taste and fancy of the speller, my lord,' replied Sam; 'I never had occasion to spell it more than once or twice in my life, but I spells it with a "V"'.

(From *The Pickwick Papers*, 1836–7, Ch. 34)

'A was an archer, and shot at a frog.' Of course he was. He was an apple-pie also, and there he is. He was a good many things in his time, was A, and so were most of his friends, except X, who had so little versatility, that I never knew him to get beyond Xerxes or Xantippe – like Y, who was always confined to a Yacht or a Yew Tree; and Z condemned for ever to be a Zebra or a Zany.

(From 'A Christmas Tree', 1850)

17

Noting the similarity

*There is a tendency for words which have similarities
in sound to be spelled in the same way. This process of
analogy affected many words that arrived in English, and
in some cases older spellings were altered to conform to
the pattern.*

At the same time as the scribes were introducing
differences in spelling, another force was making
them think in the opposite direction. This was an
awareness of the importance of showing similarities
between words – what in linguistics is technically
called *analogy*. We seem to have a built-in readiness
to think analogically in language. Young children do
it all the time when they are learning to speak: four-
year-olds say *goned* and *wented*, for example, because
they know that the usual way of forming a past tense
is to add an *-ed*, as in *walked*. It's the same with spelling. If one word looks like other similar-sounding
words in some respects, then there's pressure on us
to spell it the same in all respects. That's how children do it – until they know better.

We can see analogy operating throughout the

history of English spelling, even in tiny groups of words. Take the small set of auxiliary verbs: *would, should* and *could*. They all look the same now. But there was no *l* in *could* originally. That word was *cuðe* ('koo-thuh') in Old English. But the other two verbs both had an *l*: *wolde* and *sholde*. And when these forms developed into *would* and *should* in late Middle English, people thought there should be an *l* in *could* too – hence the modern form.

Sometimes a word is influenced by a different spelling which turns up in so many words that the pressure to change is overwhelming. This is what happened to *delight*. When it arrived in English from French it was spelled with such forms as *delit* and *delyte*. There were a few other words with the same kind of spelling variation and the same sound – (in modern spelling) *cite, site, bite, kite, quite* and *mite*. But these were a small group compared with all the words which were being spelled with *-ight*, some of which were of very high frequency in the language – *might, fight, light, right, flight, bright, height, night, sight, tight, wight, knight* ... The result was that several of the *-ite* words began to be spelled with *-ight*, and in the case of *delight* the revised spelling stayed. There was less likelihood of some of the others changing, as the difference principle operated (Chapter 16): *mite* would have clashed with *might*, *bite* with *bight*, *cite* and *site* with *sight*, and *quight* and *kight* were also being used as spellings for other words (*quit, caught*).

Analogy is the reason we have so many words

ending in /m/ followed by a silent *b*. In Old English, there were several words which ended in -*mb*, with both of the letters pronounced – *dumb, coomb, comb, climb, womb, lamb*. People stopped pronouncing the *b* at a later date: the two sounds /m/ and /b/ are both made with the two lips, and plainly it was felt that the extra effort needed to sound a *b* after an *m* was unnecessary. So a 'silent' *b* emerged. But the -*mb* spelling must have stayed prominently in mind, for we see in Middle English new words arriving that were never pronounced with a final *b*, and yet they are given one in the spelling: *plom* becomes *plumb*, *nom* becomes *numb*. And Old English words with a final *m* but lacking a *b* were affected too: we find *þuma, crum* and *lim* in Old English, but people started to spell them *thumb, crumb* and *limb*. And when *tomb* arrived in the 13th century from French *toumbe*, with a *b*, it silently followed the pattern – as did in later centuries *succumb, bomb* and *aplomb*.

Analogy is the reason we have words beginning with *wh*. In Old English, there were many words which began with the two letters the other way round: *hwa, hwit, hwilc, hwæt, hwænne, hwæl, hwistle, hwit* … Today these are all spelled with *wh*: *who, which, what, when, whale, whistle, white*. Why? Because the *hw* sequence didn't follow the pattern found in all the other words where *h* is used along with another consonant letter – *gh, sh, th* and *ch*. A *hw* looked alien, so the scribes changed it.

A similar visual process caused this pattern to

extend to *whole* and *whore*. There was no *w* in these
words in Old English: there we see *hal* and *hore*. But
the initial *wh* of other words was evidently irresistible, and we see both beginning to be spelled with *wh*
in the 15th century. It affected other words too – we
see *wholy father*, for example, in William Tyndale's
translation of the Bible in 1526 – but *holy* remained
the norm, thus avoiding any confusion with *wholly*
(also spelled *wholy* in Tyndale).

Analogy is helpful in that it usually reduces the
amount of irregularity in spelling. Occasionally,
though, it adds to it. *Build* is an example – unique
in English for its *bui* spelling, along with its deriva-
tives (*builder*, *building*, etc.). An Old English word, it
was spelled regularly in Middle English with such
forms as *bild* or *byld*. Then in the 16th century, we
find *build*. It's difficult to be sure, but one explanation is that *gui* influenced it. This spelling had
become popular in Middle English because of several
common words influenced by French, where *gu* was
a regular spelling for /g/ – *guard*, *guardian*, *guide*, *guile*,
beguile, *guinea*, *guise* … Old English words that had no
u in their spelling were influenced – *guild* and *guilt*,
both usually spelled in the modern way by around
1600. So if *guild*, why not *build*?

When *perfect* arrived in English from French in the
13th century it had no *c*. We see many spellings such
as *perfit* and *parfit*. But the related word *perfection* also
arrived at that time, and that had a very definite *c*:
early spellings include *perfeccioune* and *perfectioun*.

The stage was set for an analogy to operate, and it did – but it took a while. It was really only when Tyndale opted for the *perfect* spelling that it began to oust the other spellings of the word. And when the King James Bible used it in 1611, that settled the matter. Interestingly, people still didn't pronounce the *c* for quite some time, as shown by the continuation of spellings such as *perfet* in later writers (such as Milton) and by comments to that effect in dictionaries even as late as the 18th century.

We can never predict where analogy will operate next, or which direction it will take. Sometimes individual words influence other words in quite unexpected ways. There is an *h* in the name *Thomas* in Latin, and that is how it is spelled in Old English. There was no *h* in Latin *Antonius*, so we have *Antony* in early English, but an *h* was added to produce the usual modern spelling, *Anthony*. It must have been the prominence associated with the name *Thomas* in the Gospels which kept the *th* spelling for a /t/ sound at the forefront of people's minds. Two other words went the same way. *Thyme* arrived in English from Latin *thymum*, but was originally spelled *tyme*. The clash with *time*, also sometimes spelled *tyme*, probably motivated the introduction of the classical spelling. The name of the river that flows through London was *Temes* in Old English; it acquired its *h* analogically in the 16th century. Since then, hardly any other words have used a *th* pronounced as /t/ – just a few foreign loans, such as *thaler, Thai, thar* (a goat-antelope) and (for some people) *Neanderthal* and *apartheid*.

During the 14th century, it began to dawn on people that the spelling system was becoming unwieldy. People were beginning to get fed up with the erratic behaviour of the scribes. Geoffrey Chaucer went so far as to wish disease onto his own scribe, Adam, unless he improved his copying skills:

Adam scriveyn, if ever it thee befalle	Adam scrivener, if ever it comes to you
Boece or Troylus for to wryten newe,	To make a copy of Boece or Troilus,
Under thy long lokkes thou most have the scalle,	Under your long hair may you get scabs,
But after my makyng thou wryte more trewe;	Unless you follow my composition more accurately;
So ofte a-day I mot thy werk renewe,	Every day I often have to renew your work,
It to correcte and eek to rubbe and scrape;	To correct it and also to rub things out;
And al is thorugh thy negligence and rape.	And all because of your negligence and haste.

Things were about to improve. A standard scribal practice was growing up in the civil service domain known as Chancery. There the scribes were beginning to make selections from the many spellings available and starting to use them consistently. In their writing we see the preference for such spellings as *but* for *bot*, *not* for *nat*, *shall* for *schul* and *which* for *wich*, and we continue to use their forms today. There was still a huge amount of variation in their output, but we do get a strong sense that, at last, people were trying to do something about English spelling. The attitudes of people like Chaucer and the Chancery scribes helped to form the climate that eventually produced the accepted form of writing that today we call Standard English. And this sense of an emerging standard would soon be reinforced by the arrival of printed books. But before that happened, something else took place which would alter the character of English spelling forever. There was a seismic shift in the way words were pronounced.

Silent letters

Boss: 'How do you spell "income"? You've got here "i-n-c-u-m".'
Flapper: 'Good Heavens! How did I come to leave out the "b"?'

(Bert Thomas, from *Punch*, *c*. 1910)

18

New sounds in old letters

A series of changes in the pronunciation of long vowels took place during the late Middle English period. English spelling was significantly affected.

Say *dame* … It has a long vowel sound, as shown by the final 'silent' *e* (Chapter 6). Drop that *e* and we get a short vowel sound: *dam*. But whereas the short vowel, /æ/, is well represented by the letter *a*, the vowel sound of *dame* is odd. A long version of letter *a*, we might think, ought to sound more like 'ah' /ɑ:/, as we hear in a British version of *ma'am*, whereas in fact it is /eɪ/, more like the *e* sound we hear in a French word such as *bébé*. As the letter *a* has been used from the very beginning of English to represent /a/ sounds, as in *cat*, *fat* and hundreds more words, we might well wonder why it is now being used to represent a very different sound. What happened?

The Great Vowel Shift, in short. This is the name scholars have given to a series of changes in the pronunciation of long vowels which started around the beginning of the 15th century and went on for over 200 years. In Chaucer's time (he died in 1400), the pronunciation of the vowel in words like *dame* (and *name, gate, make* ...) was just like that in *ma'am*. That's why the scribes used the letter *a* in the first place. It worked well. But none of them could have anticipated that the vowel sound in these words was going to change so much.

What seems to have happened is that people started to say these words towards the front of the mouth. *Dame* would have begun to sound more like a long version of *dam* /dæ:m/ – much as many Americans say *ma'am* today. We don't know how long it took for the change to take place – a generation or two, probably. We can imagine old people around 1450 criticising youngsters for their new-fangled pronunciation. But it didn't stop there. Something kept the pronunciation changing and by Shakespeare's time (the later 1500s), words like *dame* were being pronounced with a sound that today we'd identify with a long version of the vowel in *them*: /dɛ:m/. Later still, it moved even higher in the mouth and became a diphthong, ending up with the sound we have today. It was all over by the 18th century. But throughout this period of change, the spelling stayed the same. *Dame* reflects the sound this word had around the year 1400.

If it had been just this vowel sound that changed, the impact on spelling would not have been great. But *all* the long vowels changed. That's why it's called a *Great* Vowel Shift. And the spelling of all words with long vowels was affected, as a result. The *i* in *mice* shows that it was once pronounced 'mees', /miːs/. The *ou* in *loud* shows that it was once 'lood', /luːd/. The *oo* in *goose* shows that it was once 'gohs', /goːs/. The *e* in *geese* shows that it was once more like 'gayce', /geːs/. The *ea* in *leaf* shows that it was once like 'lairf' (without the *r*), /lɛːf/. And the *o* in *stone* shows that it was once 'stawn', /stɔːn/.

If we put all these together into a single sentence, we hear a very different sound to what is heard today. Only a phonetic transcription can show the sounds well, but an approximate idea can be gained from seeing *geese and mice* respelled as 'gayce' and 'mees'. *A stone and a leaf* would sound more like 'a stawn and a lairf' (without the *r*). *Name a loud goose* would be close to 'nahm a lood gohs'. The spellings no longer clearly reflect the sounds.

Whether the changes were linked or separate, whether they operated in parallel or in sequence, and what caused the changes in the first place are all matters that are debated enthusiastically among linguists who study this period. But from the point of view of spelling, the effects are visible throughout the vowel system today. And once we know about the Great Vowel Shift, a number of apparent illogicalities in spelling can be explained. Why do we say *child* with a long vowel and *children* with a short vowel when both words are spelled with the same letter *i*? Because only *long* vowels were affected in the Great Vowel Shift; the short vowels stayed the same. And why do we say *entice* but *police*, *excite* but *petite, decline* but *routine,* using the one letter, *i,* for two very different sounds? In each case, the first word in these pairs was in the language before the 15th century; the second arrived later. So the first set of words had their pronunciation changed and the second group didn't. Other examples? Earlier words include *combine, shine, polite* and *recite.* Later ones include *magazine, artiste* and *unique.* Ironically, it's the second group where the letter *i* more accurately reflects Middle English speech.

The Great Vowel Shift shows the importance of vowel length in the history of English spelling. As we saw in Chapters 6 and 7, long vowels and short vowels work in very different ways, and need to be spelled differently. If all long vowels stayed long, and all short vowels stayed short, words would be a lot easier to spell. However, that's not how speech works. Over time, long vowels can become short and short ones can become long. Think of the many present-day examples where usage varies among people, illustrating such a change going on today, such as *garage* ('garahge', 'garidge'), *ate* ('ayt', 'et'), *says* ('says', 'sez'), *lichen* ('like-en', 'litchen'), *opus* ('ohpus', 'oppus'), *patent* ('paytent', 'pattent') and *privacy* ('pryvacy', 'privvacy'). All can be heard with long and short vowels. Differences between British and American English provide further examples, such as *depot* ('deppoh', 'deepoh'), *docile* ('dohsiyl', 'dossil'), *clique* ('cleek', 'clik'), *leisure* ('lezzure', 'leezure') and *progress* ('prohgress', 'proggress').

These are sporadic instances today. In earlier periods of English, changes in vowel length were much more systematic, and spelling always suffered as a consequence.

Why do vowels change their length over time? The reasons are all to do with the way a vowel relates to the other sounds within a word. How many syllables come before it and how many after it? How many consonants come before it and after it? Does it occur in a strong (stressed) syllable or not? English is a language where speakers like to keep the 'weights' of their words evenly balanced when they speak, and one way of doing this is to vary the length of the vowels.

How do we measure weight? One factor is the number of consonants a word has. We can describe the structure of a word like *room*, /ru:m/, in terms of its three sounds: consonant-vowel-consonant (CVC). This is quite a light weight compared with *limp*, which has two following consonants (CVCC), and lighter still than *glimpse* (/glɪmps/, CVCCC), and very much lighter than *glimpsed* (/glɪmpst/, CVCCCC). The more consonants there are after the vowel, the 'heavier' it gets, and we make up for that by making the vowel short. On the other hand, a simple CV sequence, or a vowel on its own, is always going to have a long sound – *me, go, do, I* …

We can see these factors playing an important part in the history of English spelling. The number of adjacent consonants can make sounds go in different directions. If a vowel has two consonants after it, it will usually be short, which is why we find *keep* (with a long vowel) and *kept* (with a short one) or *leave* and *left*. These are cases where the spelling has followed the pronunciation shift. But in cases like *dream* and *dreamt*, *lose* and *lost*, or *wise* and *wisdom*, the pronunciation has changed but the spelling has stayed the same. And if there are three following consonants, as with *children*, a short vowel is an even more likely outcome.

The number of syllables in the word affects weight too. If a vowel has two or more unstressed syllables following it, the likelihood is that it will be short. That's why we had all those examples in Chapter 9, such as *crime* (long vowel) and *criminal* (short), *type* and *typical*, and *divine* and *divinity*. The 'beat' of time it takes to say *crime* is roughly the same as the beat it takes to say *criminal*. Try saying *crime-inal*, and you'll feel the difference.

These are trends not absolute rules, and other factors can interfere with them. For example, words ending in *st* went in different directions. On the one hand we have the expected *pest*, *mist*, *cast* (for some speakers), *just*, *cost* and dozens more like them, all with short vowels; on the other hand we have quite a few words where the vowel has stayed long, such as *most*, *toast*, *priest*, *east*, *waist* and *hoist*. We would have to explore the individual words to find the factors that 'overruled' the CC effect. The issues we have been discussing earlier in this book would come into play – especially whether the vowel was long or short in its source language, and whether analogy was at work. All the modern speller needs to know is that there are some consonant clusters that need special attention, in order to anticipate such pairs as *cost* and *most* or *least* and *breast*. The *-nd* cluster is another one, with most instances short (*land, lend, spend, grand, blond, bond* ...), but some long (*find, mind, round, found* ...), leaving us with some awkward pairs, such as *friend* and *fiend* or *wind* (turn) and *wind* (breeze).

By the time printing arrived, in the 1470s, the Great Vowel Shift was well underway. The pronunciation of Chaucer was receding into the distance. Differences in accent between old and young people must have been very apparent, as well as between different parts of the country. The problem facing the scribes now was how to choose spellings that best represented speech, when sounds were changing so noticeably. And facing the printers too. In the Prologue to his translation of the *Aeneid, Eneydos*, published around 1490, William Caxton reflects on the great diversity he has found in English: 'And certainly our language now used varyeth far from that which was used and spoken when I was born ... And that common English that is spoken in one shire varyeth from another.' There's a note of frustration: 'Lo! What should a man in these days now write?' It wasn't the best of times to be a printer.

19

A printer's practice

*The arrival of printing brought a degree of order to
English orthography, compared with the diversity found
in scribal manuscripts. But variation still exists in the
earliest printed books, and sometimes printers added new
variants that actually increased spelling irregularity.*

William Caxton arrived in England in 1476, with
a pile of manuscripts, a press and sets of type, and
began work as a printer in a rented shop near the
Court in Westminster. Between then and his death
in 1491 he published over a hundred works, including Chaucer's *Canterbury Tales* and *Aesop's Fables*. By
the turn of the century, other printers were hard at
work too, such as Richard Pynson and Wynkyn de
Worde, both of whom had worked with Caxton.

It's often said that the introduction of printing
brought order to English writing. There's an element
of truth in that. The printers introduced punctuation
marks in a more systematic way. And Caxton's use
of *g* and *th* put the final nail into the coffin of the
Anglo-Saxon letters yogh, thorn and eth (Chapter
11). But as far as spelling is concerned, there was

still a large amount of variation. Caxton routinely tells his reader when he had 'finished' a book: he usually spells the word *fynysshed*, but we also find *finisshed*, *fynisshed*, *fynysshid* and *fynysshyd*. And we find many other variants, such as *Duches / Duchesse*, *musik / musycque* ('music'), *lytyl / lityl* ('little'), *wyf / wyfe* ('wife'), *good / goode, them / theym* and so on. Matters would improve as later printers developed their art and began to reflect the growing consistency seen in scribal manuscripts. But to begin with, what we see in printed books is continuing variation.

Caxton didn't seem to have been very interested in spelling. He printed what he saw, in his various manuscripts. As long as a word was recognisable, it would do. And he also made spelling suit his craft: for example, an extra letter, especially *e*, might be added to a word in order to ensure that the different lines of print came out with an even length. We find 'English' sometimes spelled as *Englyssh* and sometimes as *Englysshe*. 'Pity' might be *pity*, *pitty* or *pittye*. Having flexible spelling was a gift for printers trying to make their pages look good to the eye, with a nicely justified right-hand margin, especially if there were two columns on the page. They were reluctant to split words at the ends of lines. Their strategy was of course no different from the pragmatic decisions that had earlier been made by scribes who wanted words to be longer (as we saw in Chapter 15) or those wanting to avoid writing an alien-looking word (as with the desire to avoid a final *v* or *z:* see

Chapter 8). Adding extra letters, and especially an *e*, was a simple solution to the problem of line length.

Whatever the reason – whether added to make up a line, or reflecting a scribe's bad habits, or simply following traditional practice – Caxton's books show hundreds of words displaying a final 'silent' *e* in places where we would not expect it to be. Its usual function, as we saw in Chapter 6, is to mark a long vowel, so it isn't surprising to see it used (in his Prologue to the *Canterbury Tales*) in *grete* ('great'), *lawde* ('laud') and *saynte* ('saint'). But it is definitely out of place in *whyche* ('which'), *moche* ('much'), *gete* ('get') and *acte* ('act'). Today, many of these unnecessary *es* have been eliminated, thanks to spelling reformers such as Richard Mulcaster (Chapter 20). But we still must live with such words as *have*, *give*, *live*, *groove*, *sneeze*, *gone*, *come* and *done*. The *e* in *groove* and *sneeze* is redundant because the double vowel shows that the sound is long. And the *e* in the other words gives the wrong impression, suggesting that the vowel is long when it isn't.

In some respects, Caxton's choices made English spelling more, not less, irregular than it was already. This was certainly the case when it came to the spelling of *ghost*. Why is there an *h* here? And in *ghastly*, *aghast* and the whole family of related words – *ghostly*, *ghostliness*, *ghastliness*, *ghostbusters* and so on? It wasn't there when the word first came into English. In Anglo-Saxon England we find it used in the form *gast*, with a long 'ah' vowel. It meant a soul, a spirit, a life force. We still use the word in that sense when we talk about someone 'giving up the ghost' – either literally dying or figuratively not bothering about something any more. But there was no *h* in the Anglo-Saxon spelling: the Holy Ghost was a *Hali Gast*. Nor was there an *h* in the word in Chaucer's time. The vowel had changed by the 15th century, and had a sound more like the 'aw' of present-day *saw*. In his *Canterbury Tales*, it appears as *goost*, reflecting the long vowel. Some people spelled it as *gost*. Scottish writers showed the length of the vowel differently, as *goast* or *goist*. But no *h* anywhere.

Then along came Caxton, who sets up his printing-shop. But who was to carry out the painstaking task of typesetting the new books, letter by letter? There was nobody capable of doing it in England. Caxton had learned his trade on the European mainland, in Cologne and Bruges, so he looked to the Continent for help. We know the name of one of his assistants, Wynkyn de Worde. He and the other compositors from across the Channel all spoke Flemish.

Imagine their problem. Their English probably wasn't very good, and it was going to take them a while to make sense of the vast array of spellings used by English writers. There were no dictionaries or house style guides to help them choose which spellings to use. In Bruges they would all have been used to reading manuscripts in Flemish spelling. So, if a word reminded them of its Flemish counterpart, why not spell it in the Flemish way? The boss wouldn't mind, as long as the words were intelligible. He had more to worry about than spelling. Choosing the right manuscripts to publish, getting the books out there, and making a profit were his top priorities.

It's no surprise, then, when we read the Prologue to Caxton's *Royal Book*, printed in 1484, that we find, in a summary of the contents, a reference to the seven gifts of the *Holy Ghoost*. And we see *ghoost* again in his printing of Chaucer's *Book of Fame*, and in several other places. The Flemings had imported the *h* because in their language the word was spelled *gheest*. They probably didn't think twice about it.

It took a while for the new spelling to catch on. *Holy Gost* is what we see in the 1549 *Book of Common Prayer*. But by the end of the 16th century everyone was using the new form. Hamlet's dead father is a *ghost*, not a *gost*. And slowly the *h* spread to related words. *Aghast* appears first in the 15th century, and eventually replaces *agast*. *Ghastly* replaces *gastly*.

We should actually be thankful that so few words introduced the *h* in this way. From the typesetters' point of view, the floodgates could have opened. If *gh* worked for *ghost*, then why not also for other words beginning with the same /g/ sound? They tried. In Caxton we also find such spellings as *ghoos* for 'goose', *ghoot* for 'goat' and *gherle* for 'girl'. But none of these caught on. People must have found the *gh* too alien for everyday words. And, of course, *gh* was already being used for other sounds, as we saw in Chapter 8. Perhaps it was the more mysterious quality of *ghost* that kept the new spelling in everyone's mind for that particular word.

Where we have ghosts we have *ghouls* – an Arabic word, spelled *goul* or *goule* when it first arrived in English in the 18th century, with the *h* added later. *Gherkin* too. Nobody quite knew how to spell it, when it arrived in English from Dutch in the 16th century: we find many variants, such as *gerkin, girkin, gorkem* and *guerchin*. But one thing everybody seemed to agree about: no *h*. However, gradually the *h*-spelling started to be used, and in 1755 Dr Johnson gave it his seal of approval in his *Dictionary*. The *h* has been with us ever since.

A few other loanwords probably reinforced the trend to spell the /g/ sound in this way, especially if there was a *gh* in the source language. *Ghetto* came in from Italian with the *h* already there, so did *spaghetti*. The feeling seems to have grown that *gh* was appropriate for foreign words that had a /g/. In the 16th century, an *h* was added to German *burger* to produce *burgher* – though Americans never went down that road when the hamburger arrived 300 years later. In some cases the *h* helped to make a distinction with an already existing word: *ghee* (butter) wouldn't be confused with *gee*, nor *dinghy* with *dingy*. The *gh* words are invariably foreign-looking: *sorghum, Ghurkas, ghillie, yoghourt* ... So are the place names *Baghdad, Ghent, Afghanistan, Allegheny* ... and the people names, *Lindbergh, Haigh, Breughel, Diaghilev* ...

There have been huge rows over that final silent *h*. It's common to see a *gh* ending in British towns, such as *Edinburgh* and *Jedburgh*, so the pattern was naturally carried across the Atlantic. In 1758, Sir William Pitt was commemorated in the city of Pittsburgh in Pennsylvania. General Forbes, who chose the name, was probably thinking of Edinburgh when he spelled it, as he came from Fife in Scotland. However, in 1890, the newly established US Board of Geographic Names adopted a simplifying policy which included dropping the final *h* from all names ending in *-burgh*. Everywhere *Pittsburgh* became *Pittsburg* (see further Chapter 27). Most accepted the change; but in Pittsburgh, Pennsylvania, there was an outcry, and in 1911, after twenty years of lobbying, the *h* was restored. It's one of only three *Pittsburgh*s in the USA today, according to the Board's index. All the other towns and cities – over twenty of them – are *Pittsburg*. Not even spelling, it seems, can resist the power of the people.

An extra *h* wasn't the only sign of Dutch influence in Caxton's books. We'll also find such instances as *goed* for *good*, *ruymen* for *make room* and *vlycche* for *flitch*. These were evidently an individual typesetter's lapses, for they are well outnumbered by spellings which reflect traditional English practices. However, the point is that these spellings do exist in his books, and either nobody thought of them as errors or they didn't bother to correct them. People clearly still accepted spelling variation as a fact of life. Caxton didn't see himself as a spelling reformer. Indeed, there was no clear notion of 'spelling reform' in the 15th century. But that was about to change.

Mark Twain on spelling

There's not a vowel in the alphabet with a definite value, and not a consonant that you can hitch anything to. Look at the *h*'s distributed all around. There's *gherkin*. What are you going to do with the *h* in that? What the devil's the use of *h* in *gherkin*, I'd like to know. It's one thing I admire the English for: they just don't mind anything about them at all.

('The alphabet and simplified spelling', address given to the New York Engineers' Club, 1907)

I don't see any use in having a uniform and arbitrary way of spelling words. We might as well make all clothes alike and cook all dishes alike. Sameness is tiresome; variety is pleasing. I have a correspondent whose letters are always a refreshment to me, there is such a breezy unfettered originality about his orthography. He always spells *Kow* with a large *K*. Now that is just as good as to spell it with a small one. It is better. It gives the imagination a broader field, a wider scope. It suggests to the mind a grand, vague, impressive new kind of a cow.

(Speech at a spelling bee, reported in the *Hartford Courant*, 13 May 1875)

20

The urge to reform

By the 16th century, the amount of irregularity in English spelling had become so great that people began trying to reform it, looking out for principles that could be applied to all cases. But there were many idiosyncratic spellings, often associated with influential writers, that they could not make conform.

Spelling reform became a big issue in the 16th century, brought to a head by the huge influx of new and often strange-looking words from Latin and Greek which were coming into English as a result of the renaissance of learning in Europe. As we saw in Chapter 9, the writers of the time called them 'ink-horn' (inkpot) terms, because they contained so many letters that they used up more than their fair share of ink – words like *indeterminable*, *affability* and *ingenious*. Some presented real problems of spelling. How, for example, was *disparagement* to be spelled? Early efforts were *dispargement*, *dispergement*, *disparragement* and *disparadgment*. There must have been a feeling of 'this is the last straw'. Despite the standardising influences of the Chancery scribes and the printers, there was a real sense that the orthography was running out of control.

We can see why. Even short words were affected. Printers would add an *e* to words like *had* and *bed*, to fill up a line (as we saw in Chapter 19). These then looked like *hade* and *bede*. But their final *e* suggested a long vowel. *Bede*, for example, looked like the name of the Old English writer. Although we might think that the obvious solution was just to drop the *e*, the printers had a better idea: they could show that the vowel was short by using the double consonant principle (Chapter 7). The result: *hadde* and *bedde*. And if they then found that those words were too long for a line, the *e* could be dropped anyway, leaving *hadd* and *bedd*. We find all these spellings in late Middle English. Hundreds of words were affected – *did*, *didd* and *didde*; *sad*, *sadd* and *sadde*; *put*, *putt* and *putte*; *do*, *doe*, *doo* and *dooe* …

Richard Mulcaster is one of several writers of the time who thought things couldn't carry on like that. In his *Elementarie* (1582) he says it is a matter of national pride, apart from anything else. 'Forenners and strangers do wonder at vs,' he writes on p. 87, 'both for the vncertaintie in our writing, and the inconstancie in our letters.' He therefore lays down some rules. If there are words with too many letters – 'ignorant superfluties' (p. 105) – get rid of them. So, no consonant doubling in words like *put* and *had*. And if there are words with too few letters to express the sound well, then add what is needed. So, we should put a *t* before *ch* in words like *fetch* and *scratch*. And he loves the letter *e*. It is 'a letter of maruellous vse in the writing of our tung, and therefor it semeth to be recommended vnto vs speciallie aboue anie other letter, as a chefe gouernour in the right of our writing' (p. 112). He strongly recommends the use of an *e* that he calls 'mere silent' (i.e. 'totally silent') to distinguish *made* from *mad*, and other such words. It is the first time we see the rule for a 'silent' *e* laid down in English.

Mulcaster compiled a long list of words at the end of his *Elementarie* – in effect, an early spelling dictionary. It was a remarkably prescient list, for over half of his proposals are seen in use today. He couldn't get rid of all the anomalies, of course. He ruefully reflects at one point (p. 109), 'That to haue the most well, you must yeild to som particularities not of best reason.' And he accepts the fact that spelling is partly a matter of hard work. Rules can't explain everything, he says. We 'must leaue manie particularities to dailie practis, to be learned by oft vsing'.

No reformer could get rid of all the awkward cases. There were simply too many of them, and several had become so established by 'custom', as Mulcaster puts it, that they simply had to be left as they were. Unexpected changes in pronunciation and regional influences had led to many words developing along individual lines. The spellings, in other words, were unique. Why, for example, is *bury* pronounced 'berry'? We see it spelled thus in Middle English, along with other spellings such as *burie, birie* and *byry*. These reflect the various ways in which the word was pronounced. Evidently there was a great deal of dialect variation. The *e* spelling was used a lot in the south-east, especially in Kent, where the word would have rhymed with *merry*. The *i* spelling was more likely to reflect a northern accent. And the *u* spelling was typical of the Midlands and other parts of the south. It was the *u* version which prevailed, but – for unclear reasons – it retained a Kentish pronunciation. Maybe Chaucer was an influence. In *The Pardoner's Tale* we read (lines 883–4):

> *Now lat [let] us sitte and drynke, and make us merie,*
> *And afterward we wol [will] his body berie.*

Earlier in that tale (lines 405–6) we also see a pun on *buried* and *berried*:

> *I rekke [reckon] nevere, whan [when] that they been beryed,*
> *Though that hir [their] soules goon [go] a-blakeberyed!*

Elsewhere in *The Canterbury Tales* the word is spelled with *u*. But it is jingles like these that stay in the mind. Whatever the reason, *bury* still rhymes with *merry*, and derived words followed suit – *burial*, *burying*, *buried*, as well as several place names beginning or ending with *bury*.

And why is *busy* prounced 'bizzy'? Spellings such as *bisi*, *bisy* and *bysy* are found throughout Middle English, as well as forms with *e*, such as *besy*, and the occasional *busi*, reflecting dialect differences. The 'bizzy' pronunciation was from the East Midlands, and this became the speech norm when the dialect of that area spread south and eventually formed the basis of the standard spoken language. But *u* spellings were increasingly frequent during the 15th century, and it is *busy* which became the written standard. Why? It wasn't William Caxton this time: his preferred spelling is *e*: Sir Percival was passing a church 'where men and wymmen were besy', we read in Book 11 of his printing of Thomas Malory's *Morte d'Arthur* (1485). Nor was it Chaucer: in *The Canterbury Tales* we see only *i*, as in *bisynesse, bisy* and *bisily*. Nor was it Wycliffe's Bible translation of 1382: there's just one *u* spelling there (at Baruch 3:18); elsewhere he varies between *i* and *e*. Presumably enough *u* usage built up sporadically during the 15th century to make it the spelling of choice when William Tyndale and Myles Coverdale made their translations in the 1520s and 1530s, because in their works *u* is standard – *busye, busynes, busines, busy bodyes*. And what they did, other 16th-century biblical translations did too.

Wymmen illustrates another unique case. Why are there two pronunciations for the vowels in *woman* and *women*? In Old English, the words were *wifman* and *wifmen* – literally, 'wife-man' and 'wife-men'. The *f* sound gradually disappeared from the pronunciation. Then the *w*, with its rounded lips, exercised its influence on the vowel, so that there was a 'woo' pronunciation, soon reflected in spellings by letter *o*. But there was a problem. The stress was on the first syllable, so the second would not be clearly heard. Listen to *postman* and *postmen* in everyday Modern English speech: they sound the same. So how could the distinction between 'one woman' and 'more than one woman' be expressed, if both were pronounced /wʊmən/? Something completely unexpected happened. The plural form began to be pronounced as /wɪmɪn/, and by the end of the Middle English period we see such spellings as *wimmen* and *wymmen* appear. Why? Probably the forces of analogy again. There are several irregular plural nouns in English, and they include *goose* and *geese*, *foot* and *feet*, *tooth* and *teeth*, *child* and *children*, *brother* and *brethren*, *man* and *men*. They all have one thing in common: the vowel in the plural form is higher up in the mouth or further forward – that is, moving in the direction of /iː/. So *women* followed the trend. People used the nearest short vowel that was further forward in the mouth – and that was /ɪ/, as in *kit*.

In these and many other examples, such as *pretty*, what we observe are individual spellings that have arisen as the result of general trends in the language, but we also notice the importance of personalities. Spelling is part of fashion. If most people spell a word in a certain way, then there is pressure on you and me to do likewise. Today, the practice of 'most people' is reflected in dictionaries. But in the Middle Ages there were no dictionaries. Instead, single authors were seen as models, and Geoffrey Chaucer in particular. Thomas Hoccleve was someone who knew Chaucer, and included a portrait of him in his long poem *The Regiment of Princes* about the duties of a ruler, addressed to Henry, Prince of Wales (afterwards Henry V). Towards the end of the poem, Hoccleve addresses several stanzas to Chaucer, whom he says was his mentor. One is worth quoting in full, as it expresses the esteem in which Chaucer was held.

Allas! my worþi maister honorable,	Alas! my worthy honourable master,
This landes verray tresor and richesse,	This land's true treasure and richness,
Deþ, by thi deþ, haþ harme irreparable	Death, by your death, has irreparable harm
Unto us doon; hir vengeable duresse	Unto us done; her vindictive cruelty
Despoiled haþ þis land of the swetnesse	Has robbed this land of the sweetness
Of reþorik; for unto Tullius	Of rhetoric; for to Cicero
Was never man so lyk amonges us.	There was never a man so like among us.

Hoccleve calls him 'The first fyndere of our fair langage.'

But personalities weren't enough. People wanted principles. And in the 16th century, reformers thought they had found one: etymology.

George Bernard Shaw on spelling

The English have no respect for their language, and will not teach their children to speak it. They spell it so abominably that no man can teach himself what it sounds like. It is impossible for an Englishman to open his mouth without making some other Englishman hate or despise him.

(From the Preface to *Pygmalion*, 1913)

21

Remembering Latin

*During the 16th century, people increasingly turned
to etymology as a way of explaining and regularising
English spelling. Many 'silent letters' were the result.*

During the 16th century, spelling reform became a
live issue. We've already seen some of the ways in
which scribes and printers had tried to cope with
English spelling – finding patterns, encountering
exceptions to the patterns, discovering exceptions to
the exceptions ... But by the 1500s, many writers felt
things had gone too far. It wasn't enough to just let
the spelling evolve naturally, they said, with individuals making personal decisions about how to spell
words and then leaving it up to the unpredictable
forces of everyday usage to decide which spellings
would catch on. There had to be a better way. There
were just too many variations around, as we saw
with *night* (Chapter 15).

Various kinds of spelling reform were proposed.
They included tweaking existing spellings, cutting
out unnecessary letters and inventing new ones.
Some writers thought the best thing to do was

get rid of everything and start all over again with a brand-new alphabet. Writers such as John Hart, William Bullokar and Alexander Gill penned large treatises about the writing system and how it might be 'emended'. There was a real concern to find good 'reasons' to justify what needed to be done.

And one of these reasons was to make more use of Latin. We've already seen (Chapter 10) something of its prestige and influence. It was a language which all educated people knew. Children in grammar school were immersed in it. They had to speak it as well as write it, and they did so every day of the school week. So, if English spelling was a mess, and all literate people knew Latin, why not put Latin to work to help reduce some of the uncertainties in English? It seemed like a very good idea.

Take the anonymous author of *The Writing Scholar's Companion*, published in 1695. It is subtitled: *Infallible Rules for Writing with Ease and Certainty*, and one of those rules deals with 'silent consonants'. These, he says, 'must be written', and one of the reasons he gives is 'to discover their original derivation, as debt from debitum, the Latin word doubt from dubius'. In this, he was following a way of thinking about spelling that had developed over a century before.

Debt is the classic case to illustrate what had happened. English borrowed this word from French *dette* in the early Middle Ages. The earliest citations in the *Oxford English Dictionary* are in the 13th century, and the word has various spellings – *det, dett, dette, deytt*. They have one thing in common: no *b*. Nothing much wrong with *det*, you might think. But during the 16th century some writers had other ideas.

They thought like this. If a word comes ultimately from Latin, let's see if there's anything in the Latin spelling that would help fix it in the English mind. The Latin source of *det/dett/dette/deytt* is *debitum*. So, someone reasoned (we have no idea who was the first to suggest this), if we add a *b*, this will be very helpful. It won't affect the way we speak; people will carry on saying /det/. The *b* can be a 'silent letter'. But it will be a useful mnemonic when people have to write the word. It will avoid them puzzling over whether the correct spelling is *det*, *dett*, *dette* or *deytt*.

Today, with most people lacking Latin, and silent letters seen as a hindrance rather than a help, this seems like the craziest of decisions. But the 16th-century mindset was very different. People accepted the change, and valued it. The new spelling appeared in prestigious publications. The first recorded use of it in the *Oxford English Dictionary* is 1549, in *The Book of Common Prayer*: in the office for visitation of the sick, the sick person is asked to 'declare his debtes'. The 1557 Geneva Bible has the same spelling. And, although there are sporadic earlier spellings, by 1600 it had become the norm. In Shakespeare's First Folio (1623), the word turns up forty-three times, always spelled *debt*. The only time we see it referred to as *det* is when the pedant Holofernes, in *Love's Labour's Lost*, insists that because there is a *b* in the spelling it should be pronounced. He can't stand such 'rackers of orthography' as Don Armado, he says, who 'speak *dout* sine [without] *b* when he should say *doubt, det* when he should pronounce *debt* – *d, e, b, t* not *d, e, t*'. 'It insinuateth me of insanie,' says Holofernes. It drives him mad!

Doubt had the same sort of history as *debt*: it had such spellings as *dute* and *doute* in Middle English, then a *b* was introduced from Latin *dubitare*. Holofernes would have given it a warm welcome. During the 16th century, etymology ruled. *Subtle* got its *b* from *subtilis* (earlier spellings were *sotill, sutell*, etc.). *Indict* got its *c* from *dictare* (earlier *endite, indite*, etc.), *arctic* from *arcticus* (earlier *artik, artyke*, etc.), and *victuals* from *victualis* (earlier *vitaile, vitayle*, etc.). *Receipt* got its *p* from *recepta* (earlier *recyt, resseit*, etc.). *Account* got a *p* from *computare* (*accompt* – earlier spellings were *acunt, acont*, etc.), and the *p* stayed until such time as the pronunciation moved away from a potentially embarrassing ambiguity with the *c*-word. *Myrrh* got its *h* from *myrrha* (earlier *murra, mirra*, etc.). *Salmon* got its *l* from *salmo* (earlier *samoun, sammon*, etc.); *balm* from *balsamum* (earlier *bawm, bame*, etc.); *falcon* from *falco* (earlier *faukun, faucoun*, etc.); *fault* from *fallitus* (earlier *faut, fawt*, etc.) and *assault* from *assultus* (earlier *assaut, assawte*, etc.). In some cases, the new consonant eventually came to be pronounced, as in *fault* and *arctic*. The *h* pronounced in modern *habit* was a Latin addition too, from *habitus* (earlier *abit, abyt*, etc.).

In Middle English we see *very* spelled as *verray*, as we would expect for a short vowel, but classically minded writers preferred a version that looked like Latin *verum*, with just one *r*. We might expect *abhor* to be spelled *abhore*, like other words ending in this sound, such as *adore* and *ignore*; but if you know your Latin, you know that *abhor* comes from a different class of verb. The origin of *ignore* is *ignorare* with an -*are* ending; *adore* is the same, *adorare*. But the origin of *abhor* is *horrere*, with an -*ere* ending. So obviously we should spell it differently.

These are straightforward examples of the influence of Latin. There's a more complex background for words like *author* and *authority*. *Author* started life in English as a borrowing from French with such spellings as *autor* and *autour*; *authority* was the same, with *autorite* and *autoryte*. There was no *h* in the French words, and none in the original Latin either – *auctor* and *auctoritas* – so where did it come from? It was probably one of those cases where writers saw a similar-looking word and assumed that these words were spelled in the same way. Analogy again. But which one?

The most likely candidate is *authentic*. All three words were coming into English at around the same time (14th century). *Authentic* too was being written without an *h* – we find such spellings as *autentik*, *attentik* and *awtentyke*. But here the original Latin was *authenticus*, using a *th*, which was the way the Romans wrote the word when they borrowed it themselves from Greek. So in due course the Latin-aware writers inserted it into the English word, and from there it spread. If *authentic* had an *h*, so should *authority* and *author*. There was even a similarity of meaning to support a link: if something is 'authentic' it has a certain 'authority' about it because produced by a genuine 'author'. The *h* stayed – and eventually became part of the pronunciation. Today, most people say *authority* with a 'th' sound (/θ/). (In Shakespeare's day it would have been a /t/ – similar to what we still hear in some modern accents, such as Irish English.)

But, we might think, if *author* and *authority* came from *auctor* and *auctoritas*, why didn't the *c* come into English as well? The answer, of course, is that it did. Among the earliest English spellings of these two words are *auctor* and *auctorite*. And the link between the three words I've been discussing was apparent again, as an extra *c* was sometimes added to *authentic* too: *auctentyke*. Along comes the *h*, and for a while we see forms containing both, such as *aucthor* and *aucthority*. But now people were faced with a pronunciation problem: pronouncing *ct* /kt/ involves quite a tricky tongue movement – first the back of the tongue makes contact with the roof of the mouth and then, very rapidly, the front of the tongue. The stage is set for a simplification – and this is what happened. People didn't pronounce the *c*. It's a simplification we sometimes see in other words. Americans don't pronounce the *c* before *t* in *Connecticut*.

Lots of people don't pronounce the *c* in *adjunct*. And eventually, *c* got dropped from the spelling.

This consonant combination isn't the only one that simplifies because of difficult pronunciation: *autumn* and *hymn* (from Latin *autumnus* and *hymnus*) lost their final /n/ sound for the same reason, but in these cases the letter stayed in the spelling. There were *ns* also in the Latin origins of *condemn*, *solemn*, *column* and *damn*. Analogy sometimes pulled these words in different directions. *Column* is a good example. We've come across that vowel + *m* pronunciation before (in Chapter 17), in relation to such words as *dumb*. There we see a silent *b*. And so it's not surprising to find that, for a while in the history of some of these words, they *were* also spelled in this way, as seen in *columb* and *damb*. But in the 16th century, the feeling must have been that a silent *n* ending was better because it reflected the Latin sources (*columnus, damnare*). The *n* was also being pronounced in related words, such as *columnary* and *damnation*. There was no contest. All other spellings – *collum, collume*, etc. – soon died out.

The Latinists didn't always get it right, however. Why do we have an *s* in *island*? The word appears in Old English as *iland* or *igland* – from *ey* + *land*. An *ey* was a Germanic way of describing a piece of land surrounded by water – the same word turns up in Old Norse and Old Frisian – and we see it today at the end of the county name *Anglesey*. The Anglo-Saxon word carries over into Middle English, but then gets confused with another word, *isle*, which had come in from French: *ile* (pronounced 'eel'). The English weren't the only spellers to be influenced by Latin, it seems. The French were too, for they had begun to write *ile* as *isle*, influenced by the Latin origin of the word, *insula*. This evidently impressed printer William Caxton, who uses the spellings *isle* and *ysle* in some of his books.

Things might have stayed that way: *iland*, with no *s*, and *isle*, with a silent *s*. But people then associated the two words in their mind and began to think of *iland* in a different way. It sounded like *ile* + *land*. If so, they thought, then the first part should be spelled like *isle*. And this is how *island* got its *s*. It was a mistake – the kind of mistake that often happens in the history of English, when people mis-analyse a word. The word for *apron* was *napron* when it arrived in English (from French *naperon*), but after people encountered the phrase *a napron*, they heard it as *an apron*, and that's how it stayed.

Island wasn't the only example of classical influence that went wrong. Why is there an *sc* in *scissors*? Because spelling enthusiasts thought that it came from the Latin word *scindere* 'to cut'. In fact, it comes from *cisorium*, 'cutting instrument'. If the Latin were being accurately reflected, it should be spelled *cissors*. And why is there an *sc* in *scythe*? Same reason, though in this case the word comes from an Old English word *siðe* ('see-thuh'). And why is there a *p* in *ptarmigan*? This is a Scottish Gaelic word, *tarmachan*, which came into English spelled *tarmaken* or *termagant*. But in the 17th century people thought it was a Greek word, and that the beginning must be from *ptero-*, meaning 'wing-shaped, feathered', so they added the *p*. (The Greek source is correct in *pterodactyl* and *helicopter*.)

During the Renaissance, people had long memories when it came to spelling. They remembered their Latin – or thought they did. And etymological reasoning increasingly became a major factor in decision-making over spelling. We can't explain some of the famous difficulties in English spelling without it.

22

More etymologies

Etymology explains many of the notorious confusable words in English spelling, as the confused words have different languages of origin. Silent letters also often reflect an earlier period in language history.

Etymology lies behind many common spelling errors. Anyone who spells *privilege* as *privilidge* shows they have learned the normal rule for representing a final /ʤ/ sound in an English word (Chapter 5); but they haven't taken into account the etymology. They aren't the first to have a problem with this word. With over 120 variant spellings for it recorded in the *Oxford English Dictionary*, it's one of the most diversely spelled words in the history of English. Dr Johnson followed the Latin source word, *privilegium*, and we have had *privilege* ever since. *Sacrilege* and *sacrilegious* went the same way. And it's thanks to the influence of Latin that we use *cede* in such words as *concede*, *recede* and *precede*, instead of the more traditional English way seen in *succeed* and *proceed*.

If an unusual spelling turns up in several words, the reason will be that they all come from the same language. French spellings regularly illustrate this point. Words with a silent *g* before *n* all come from French, or Latin via French, as with *deign, benign, sign, align* and *feign*. The *ui* of *nuisance* is seen again with the same vowel sound in such words as *fruit, juice* and *recruit*. Even Old English words were affected. *Bruise,* for example, appears in Old English as *brysan,* and developed in Middle English in such forms as *brise* and *bruse*. Left to itself, it would eventually have emerged in Modern English as *brise* (rhyming with *wise*). But it wasn't left to itself. At some point in the 15th century, it fell under the influence of French *bruisier*.

When two consonants have different spellings but the same pronunciation, the reason is often etymological. Why do we spell *scorn* with *sc* and *skin* with *sk*? Words from French, Latin and Greek usually end up with *sc* (*scorn, scarce, scourge*); but if they come from Old Norse or Dutch we see the spelling used in those languages, resulting in (Norse) *skin* and *sky* or (Dutch) *skate* and *skipper*. There have been periods of uncertainty for some words, and some variant usage. *Skeleton* was originally *sceleton*; *sceptic* became *skeptic* in American English. But on the whole, the spellings indicate the source language clearly.

Sometimes two languages get brought together in a quite unpredictable way. Why is *nephew* pronounced with a /v/? The word is from French *neveu,* and when it arrived in the 14th century we find such spellings as *nefew* or *neueu,* which is what we would

expect. (The *f* was pronounced /v/, as we saw in
Chapter 14.) But a century later, people tried to link
it to the Latin source word for nephew, *nepos*. They
borrowed the *p*, and suddenly we see such spellings
as *nepvew*. A *pv* sequence in English writing looked
really alien, so it was respelled as *ph*. But by then
the /v/ pronunciation had come to be established,
and so we find the anomaly. It's an anomaly, though,
which may be on its way out, for during the 19th
century the *ph* became increasingly sounded as /f/.
It's the majority pronunciation today.

In some cases, the spelling difference is much
more complex. The evidence about the relative influence of French and Latin is frequently ambiguous.
Words have often changed their spelling over time,
influenced first by one language and then by the other,
and in such cases we have no choice but to follow the
fortunes of the individual words. The many words
ending in *-ent* or *-ant* illustrate this situation. They
are characterised by a great deal of inconsistency, as
we see in such pairs as *dependant* (noun) and *depen-
dent* (adjective) or *attendant* and *superintendent*. These
are the famous 'confusables', known especially for
the way they can trip up contestants in spelling bees,
but they present all English learners with a problem.

The confusion usually arises in the unstressed
part of a word. Why do we have such difficulty distinguishing *stationary* and *stationery*? Because in
normal colloquial speech there is no difference in
the sound of the two endings: the emphasis is on the

first syllable, and the vowels in the remaining syllables are pronounced less distinctly. The two spellings reflect different origins. The ending in *stationary* comes from Latin *-arius*; we see it again in such words as *necessary*, *primary* and *contrary*. The ending in *stationery* comes from French *-erie*; we see it again in *cutlery*, *pottery* and *confectionery* – and especially today in a raft of new coinages, such as *eatery* and *winery*. The same kind of etymological explanation accounts for the many pairs of words distinguished by a single vowel in an unstressed syllable, such as (the stressed syllables are underlined) *compli̱mentary* vs. *complemeṉtary*, *pri̱nciple* vs. *pri̱ncipal*, *cu̱rrent* vs. *cu̱rrant* and *allu̱sion* vs. *illu̱sion*. (How to handle these in teaching is discussed in Appendix I.)

Just as problematic for the speller are the words which derive from different types of Latin verb. Why do we have *spatial* and *facial* or *initial* and *beneficial*? Words ending in *-cial* go back to a French or Latin word where there was a *c* in the spelling; those with *-tial* have a source with a *t* in the spelling. Why do we have *admirable* and *audible*? Because *admirable* comes from a verb ending in Latin spelled with an *a* (*admirare*, pronounced 'ad-mi-ra̱h-ray') , and *audible* comes from one spelled with an *i* (*audire*, pronounced 'ow-de̱e-ray'). In Latin, the different vowels were emphasised, and in earlier English this was also often the case. Not so now. And as the pronunciation contrast diminished so the spelling confusion increased.

Silent letters also usually have an etymological

explanation. In some cases, an extra letter has been added to show a classical origin, as we saw in words like *debt* (Chapter 21). A common occurrence is to find the silent letter arriving as part of a loanword, such as with *fracas* or *khaki* (more on this in Chapter 33). Sometimes it is there as a result of a change in pronunciation – which is how the most familiar examples of silent letters arose. Most are the result of the changes that took place between Old and Middle English. All letters were pronounced in Old English, as we saw in Chapter 4, so when we see such forms as *write* and *wreak*, we are seeing a pronunciation pattern that was very much alive a thousand years ago. It was the same with words beginning with *gn* (as in *gnaw* and *gnat*) and *cn* (as in *knee* and *knife* – the French scribes replaced the *c* with a *k*). And in words like *answer* and *sword* the *w* was originally sounded.

Some of these consonant pairs feel uncomfortable today. It's not that English speakers are unable to pronounce a sequence of *g* + *n* or *k* + *n*. We do it easily when a syllable ending in *g* or *k* is followed by one beginning with *n*, as in *acknowledge* and *agnostic*. And we have no difficulty in pronouncing these sequences at the beginning of a word if we want to – as when people deliberately say the words in a funny way as *k-nife* or *g-nash*. Flanders and Swann's famous phonetic manipulation of *gnu* as *g-nu* in their 'Gnu Song' is a perfect illustration. But today these clusters feel alien, and we avoid them even with modern loanwords, such as *gnostic* and *gneiss*. Similarly,

English speakers evidently don't like a sequence of *m* + *n* or *n* + *w* at the beginning of a word – which is why we say *mnemonic* without its initial /m/ (as in the original Greek) and *nuisance* as /nju:/ not as /nwi:/ (as it would have been in the original French).

Silent letters also provide us with what is probably the most famous example of spelling difficulty in English: the *-ough* problem. And here, too, etymology forms a large part of the explanation.

A word I always misspell

Answering the question 'Is writing your novels pleasure or drudgery?'

Pleasure and agony while composing the book in my mind; harrowing
irritation when struggling with my tools and viscera – the pencil that
needs resharpening, the card that has to be rewritten, the bladder that
has to be drained, the word that I always misspell and always have to
look up … questionnaires – a word whose spelling I have to look up
every time.

(From Vladimir Nabokov, *Strong Opinions*, 1973, pp. 145, 178)

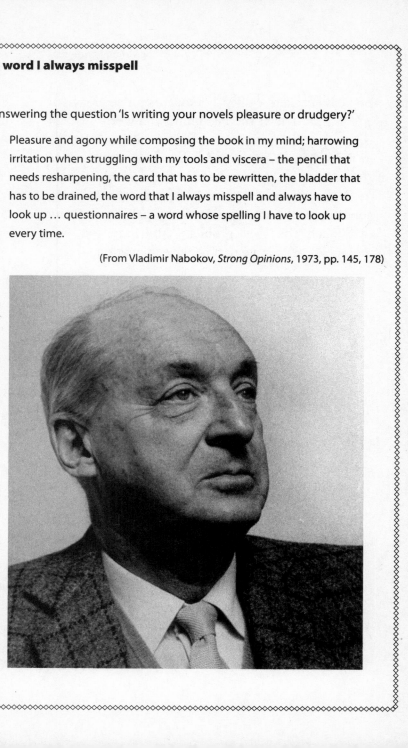

23

Famous spellings

Even the most notorious of spelling difficulties, such as the ough *set, can be explained through etymology. It turns out that not all of the problem cases are equally irregular.*

Etymology is an essential perspective if we want to explain the spellings that have achieved notoriety in English. The *ough* set would probably come out as top of any hate list, and when we see the kind of creative juxtapositions illustrated in Chapter 1 ('Though the rough cough and hiccough plough me through, I ought to cross the lough') it's easy to understand why. But what caused this extraordinary family gathering? And is it really as irregular as people think?

Although we can view all the *ough* words side by side now, that wasn't how it started. They arrived in English at different times over several hundred years. The story begins in Old English, where one of the sound values of letter yogh was /x/, as we saw in Chapter 5. Words like *niȝt, hiȝ, burȝ, miȝt* and *thoȝ* were respelled by French scribes with a *gh*, so we get *night, high, burgh, might* and *though* as common spellings for these words in early Middle English. To begin with, the *gh* continued to be pronounced. When we read in the opening lines of *The Canterbury Tales* about the little birds sleeping all through the 'nyght', we need to take that spelling at face value, and read it as /nɪxt/, with the 'ch' sound of Scots *loch* or Welsh *bach*. But the /x/ disappeared from southern English during the 15th and 16th centuries. North of the border, and in some other provincial accents, it stayed – hence modern Scots spellings such as *moonlicht nicht*.

It was an important group of words. Some of them, such as *might* (as in *I might see*), *ought, through, though* and *naught*, were high frequency. And when a group of these words rhyme, they influence others through the power of analogy (Chapter 17). *Might, night, fight, fright, sight* ... We have already seen how *delight* gained its *gh* because people treated it in the same way. The same thing happened to *sprightly*: it is from *sprite*, a variant form of *spirit*. There was no *gh* in this word when it arrived in English from French (*esprit*). Similarly, *haughty* arrived from French in the 16th century, with its root originally spelled *haut* (meaning 'high'), but the 'aw' pronunciation suggested a parallel with such words as *caught* and *taught* – hence *haughty*. *Distraught* did the same. *Inveigh* followed *weigh*.

There used to be far more *gh* spellings in English. In Shakespeare's First Folio we find such examples as *spight* ('spite') and *despight* ('despite'), *willough* ('willow'), *yaughan* ('yawn'), and the fascinating *bowgh wawgh* ('bow-wow'). It's also easy to see that the printers were finding *gh* as problematical then as we do today. Should a word be spelled with a *w* or a *gh*? If in doubt, it seems, use both. And so we find *plowgh'd* ('ploughed'/'plowed'), *showghes* ('shows'), *hewgh* ('hew'), *slawghter* ('slaughter') and *nawghty* ('naughty'). Any of these spellings might have caught on. People who complain about *gh* spellings today don't know how lucky they are! There could have been far more.

The irregularity in all these cases has been blamed on *gh*. But in fact *gh* is behaving perfectly regularly here: it is silent. It's the vowels that are the problem – not so much with *i* or *ei*, because the *i* of *right*, *might*, *sigh*, etc. is exactly the same as the *i* of *rite*, *I*, *mine* and many more, and the *ei* of *eight*, *sleigh*, *neighbour*, etc. is exactly the same as the *ei* of *vein*, *veil*, *reign* and others. The nuisance is the way *ou* has come to be used to represent several sounds. We have the /aʊ/ sound of *plough* and *bough*, the /ɔ:/ sound of *ought* and *bought*, the /əʊ/ sound of *dough* and *though*, the /ə/ sound of *borough* and *thorough*, and the /u:/ sound of *through*. That's why <u>ough</u> is the sequence that looms large in any discussion of *gh* irregularity.

However, when we compare these word-sets with others that share the *ou* vowel spelling we see that they are not equally irregular. The vowel sound in *bough, plough, drought* and *doughty* actually chimes with many other words, such as *round, bounce, ouch* and *mountain*. If you know that *ou* is normally pronounced /aʊ/ and *gh* is normally silent, you shouldn't have any problem with these. It's the others that are the real exceptions. There are hardly any chimes here, apart from some specialised terms and proper names, such as *naughty / Taunton, though / furlough, thorough / Willoughby, through / Hugh*.

We also have to count as real exceptions the few cases where the *gh* isn't silent. I've already discussed one group of these, in Chapter 11. This was the pronunciation shift that took place in the 15th century. The /x/ became /f/, giving us *enough, laugh, tough, draught, chough* and *cough*. In the case of *dwarf*, found in Middle English in such forms as *dwargh* and *dwergh* as well as *dwerff* and *dwarf*, the spelling eventually followed the pronunciation. And in one instance we find both spellings retained as different senses developed: *draught* and *draft*.

That leaves *hiccough* and *lough*. These are the two really exceptional cases. *Hiccough* wasn't always spelled this way. When it arrived in the 16th century, it was written in such forms as *hikup* and *hickop*, as well as *hicket* and *hickock* (a 'little hic'). However, a popular feeling arose that there was a connection with a *cough*. So, people reasoned, if *cough* was spelled with *ough*, *hiccough* should do the same. Analogy again – but the earlier pronunciation stayed.

Lough is exceptional for a different reason: it

reflects the pronunciation of another language – in this case, Gaelic. It's pronounced with a final /x/ – and thus, ironically, is actually closer to Old English than any of the other words in the *gh* group. We see a similar sound in a few proper names, such as *McLoughlin* and *Noughty*. But most names have evolved a more phonetic spelling over the centuries, such as *Ainscough* becoming *Ainscow* (as *plough* has become *plow* in American English). *Lough* itself is now restricted to Irish names; it's spelled *Loch* in Scotland.

It's because *ough* spellings in English are of several different types that it isn't helpful to bring them together. It may be fun to create such sentences as 'Though the rough cough ...' but it's highly misleading, as it suggests that all *ough* spellings are 'equally irregular', whereas some are clearly more systematic than others. The same point applies to the use of the phrase 'silent letters' as a comment about the general character of English spelling. Yes, English has many silent letters, but they perform a host of functions, some of which are highly regular (such as marking long vowels, as we saw in Chapter 6) and some of which are irregular.

In cases like those discussed in the last two chapters, etymology explains why there is a problem, but it provides no teaching solution, especially today, when classical languages are not a routine part of the school curriculum. So where are solutions to be

found? One thing the 16th-century spelling reformers did, which often passes unnoticed, is that they
began the practice of teaching people how to remember their recommendations. The search for rules was
on.

24

Spelling 'rules'

*People put their faith in simple spelling 'rules', learned
in isolation, but these always fail to work, partly because
there are too many exceptions, and partly because the
explanation necessarily involves other aspects of language,
such as pronunciation and grammar. The famous 'i before
e' rule provides an illustration.*

In 1580, the reformer William Bullokar published
a *Short Introduction or Guiding to Print, Write, and
Reade Inglish Speech*. He uses a question-and-answer
approach, and several of his rules are in rhyming
couplets or quatrains – like his opening one (I modernise his idiosyncratic spelling):

*Question: What rules are there for spelling?
1 Note vowels, half vowels, and diphthongs also,
In every word, syllables to know.*

Over fifty more verses follow. And rhyming mne-
monics have been part of classroom practice ever
since.

Two hundred years later, we see the most influential of all the prescriptive grammarians, Lindley

Murray, include a chapter on 'Words in general, and the rules for spelling them' in his *English Grammar* (1795). His rules are couched in a more pedestrian prose, but they have the same intent as Bullokar's. They also illustrate the 'exceptions within exceptions' kind of statement which has always bedevilled the teaching of spelling, such as his rule two:

> Monosyllables ending with any consonant but f, l, or s, and preceded by a single vowel, never double the final consonant: excepting add, ebb, butt, egg, odd, err, inn, and buzz.

It's difficult to work out just what the rule does apply to – and whether it is a real rule at all, if it needs eleven qualifications to make it work. Some writers acknowledged the problem. In the preface to his *American Spelling Book*, published soon after Murray's book, Noah Webster was unequivocal:

> Rules are of no consequence but to printers and adults. In Spelling Books they embarrass children, and double the labour of the teacher.

He had been a teacher, and knew what he was talking about.

Why don't rules work? Partly because history has produced so many exceptions, but also because spelling has been viewed in isolation from the rest of language. Spelling, however, is an integral part of language, and its forms can be understood only if we see the way they interact with the forces that come from pronunciation, grammar and word-building.

We cannot solve the problem of spelling without knowing something about how the rest of language works.

The most famous spelling rule in the English language provides an illustration. Generations of children have been taught a rule which, in one early spelling book, went like this: '*i* before *e*, except after *c*; and, if you please, the little word *seize*'. If you picked up a different primer, it might look like this: '*i* before *e*, except after *c*, or when sounded like *a*, as in *neighbour* and *weigh*'. There are several other variants.

Spelling jingles of this kind go back centuries, but the *ei / ie* rule is quite recent, becoming very popular in schools only during the 19th century. It could have arisen only after spelling had stabilised and the demand for correctness entered classrooms. Earlier, spelling was too uncertain and changing for such a rule to be of any help. For example in 1582, Richard Mulcaster spells *friend* as *frend* and *clemency* as *clemencie*, notes that *straight* interchanges with *streight*, and recommends *yeild* and *feild* alongside *eight* and *weight*. Two hundred years later, the situation was much clearer. The spellings in Dr Johnson's *Dictionary* (1755) show that the modern use of *ei* and *ie* was largely established, with just a few remaining differences (such as *wiery* for *wiry*), and he draws attention to both of the *ei* and *ie* letter sequences in his Introduction.

The 18th century was an era when people realised they had to get their spelling right – adults as well as children. Lord Chesterfield was typical of his age in seeing spelling as the true mark of an educated gentleman. On 19 November 1750 he writes, replying to a letter from his son:

> I come now to another part of your letter, which is the orthography, if I may call bad spelling *orthography*. You spell induce, *enduce*; and grandeur, you spell grand*ure*; two faults, of which few of my house-maids would have been guilty. I must tell you, that orthography, in the true sense of the word, is so absolutely necessary for a man of letters, or a gentleman, that one false spelling may fix a ridicule upon him for the rest of his life; and I know a man of quality, who never recovered the ridicule of having spelled *wholesome* without the *w*.

The same attitude could be found in America. Thomas Jefferson writes to his daughter Martha on 28 November 1783:

> Take care that you never spell a word wrong. Always before you write, consider how it is spelled, and, if you do not remember, turn to a dictionary. It produces great praise to a lady to spell well.

In such a climate, the search for rules became a priority – but writers quickly discovered that it wasn't easy. Lindley Murray also mentions the difference between *ei* and *ie*, and talks about the sounds they represent, though he doesn't go so far as to formulate a rule about their use. Maybe he saw the difficulty! But most schoolteachers weren't so cautious.

We don't know who first cooked up the '*i* before *e*' rule, but the enticing simplicity of the rhyme persuaded everyone that it was really useful. And it became the rule to be remembered above all others. Indeed, for some it became a symbol of a whole pedagogical approach, as we see in the title of Judy Parkinson's 2007 book: *I Before E (Except After C): Old-School Ways to Remember Stuff*.

Of course, as generations of children have repeatedly discovered, the rule doesn't work. It was a typical example of something we see often in the history of language. People notice a linguistic point (in this case, how to remember the difference between such words as *believe* and *receive*), find some examples which seem to support it, and then generalise wildly. They notice cases where the rule doesn't apply, and call them 'exceptions', but they don't think to find out how many exceptions there are, and they don't try to explain them. Over time, the exceptions build up until sometimes they outnumber the cases covered by the rule. People start to complain about it, but by then it's too late: the rule has become part of the establishment.

The original linguistic point was a sensible one: the norm is indeed '*i* before *e*'. The historical processes we've been talking about in this book have resulted in hundreds of words which are spelled with *ie* – not only everyday words, but many names of people, places and objects. The usual sound that *ie* represents is /i:/, as we see and hear in *achieve, believe, grieve, retrieve, field, grief, thief, belief, piece, shriek, diesel, genie, Brie, Gielgud* and many more. Sometimes other sounds are represented, such as the /ɪə/ of *alien, audience* and *spaniel* or the /aɪ/ of *pie, die* and *lie*. In a few cases the two letters each represent a sound – /aɪə/ in *client, quiet, science* and *anxiety*, or /iːe/ in *siesta, serviette, concierge* and *Vienna*. In *view, lieu* and *adieu*, the sound is /juː/. And in the solitary case of *friend*, it is /e/. But *ie* = /iː/ is undoubtedly the norm.

And this is the point to note if we are trying to make the rule work. If we listen to the way we say the main class of so-called 'exceptions' to the rule, we notice something straightaway. These too are all pronounced /iː/: *deceive, perceive, ceiling, conceit, conceive, receipt* and *receive*, along with all their derived forms (*conceiving, misconceive,* etc.). At the very least, the rule would have to be '*i* before *e* except after *c*, when the spelling represents /iː/'). But that's not enough to handle all the exceptions.

The *ie* visual pattern was reinforced when this spelling appeared as the result of something going on in English grammar. As we saw in Chapter 15, nouns ending in *y* become *ies* in the plural (*party > parties*); verbs ending in *y* become *ies* in the third person and *ied* in the past tense (*cry > cries, cried*); adjectives ending in *y* change their form in the comparative and superlative (*happy, happier, happiest*). This means that an *ie* spelling is never very far away in a piece of writing.

The important thing to note about suffixes is that

they are added to words on the basis of the meaning people want to express. The letter the words happen to end with is a side-issue. So we form the plural of *baby, body, lily, lorry, daisy* and so on by simply changing the *y* to *ies*, regardless of the fact that these endings have respectively a preceding *b, d, l, r* and *s*. And if the noun happens to end in *c* before the *y*, then that will stay too – hence *agencies, policies, lunacies, vacancies, fallacies, democracies* and many more. There are also a few adjectives and verbs in the same group (*racier, pricier, juiciest, fancied* ...). So, if we wanted to keep the rule, we would have to add something like '*i* before *e* except after *c*, unless that *c* appears before an ending which shows a change in the form of a noun, verb or adjective'.

The same principle obtains when we build up words by adding a suffix, as in *consist, consistent, consistently, consistence, consistency* ... Here, the root of the word happens to end in a *t*. But what if it ends in a *ce*, as in *suffice*? Now we get *sufficient, sufficiency, sufficience, sufficiently* ... And when we think of all the words that have these endings after *c*, we can see that quite a large number of 'exceptions' are involved: *ancient, efficiency, conscience, proficient* ... So now we would have to add to the rule something like '*i* before *e* except after *c*, unless that *c* appears before an ending which builds up a larger word'.

We can now turn to the other big group of 'exceptions' – those where we get *ei* without a preceding *c*. These are a small group by comparison with those in *ie.* Most of them show the influence of French spelling, which the scribes kept when the words were borrowed into English in the Middle Ages. There was some variation at the time between *ei* and *ai* (or *ey* and *ay*) spellings for these words, which lasted for a while before the *ei* form prevailed. That's why we have *forfeit* (French spelling *forfait*), *heinous* (*haineux*), *leisure* (*leisir*), *seize* (*seisir*), *vein* (*veine*), *veil* (*veile*), *beige* (*beige*), *rein* (*rein*), *heir* (*heir*) and *reign* (*reigne*). *Reign* is particularly interesting, as it seems to have been the model for *sovereign* (*souverein*) – which incidentally picked up its *g* in the 15th century – and *foreign* (*forain*), which added its *g* in the 16th. In modern times, we see French influence again in several scientific terms, such as *codeine* and *protein*.

If we are aware of how French spelling affected English, we could argue that none of these examples are really exceptions after all. But there's no arguing that for *weird*, which is indeed weird. It was *wyrd* in Old English, where it meant 'fate' or 'destiny'. It emerges in Middle English especially as an adjective in the phrase *weird sisters*, where it refers to women who can control human destiny – that is, the Fates, and is especially well known in Shakespeare's *Macbeth* (I. 3. 32–4), where the three witches describe themselves in that way:

> *The Weird Sisters, hand in hand,*
> *Posters of the sea and land,*
> *Thus do go, about, about …*

(In this context we have to remember to ignore the modern meaning of 'odd' for *weird*, which is a 19th-century development.) Typical Middle English spellings are *wird* and *werd*. The first sign of an *ie* is in the 16th century, where we find both *weird* and *wierd*, especially in texts coming from Scotland. It looks as if the unusual spelling of *weird* is an example of Scottish influence. And *weird* may have influenced the spelling of *weir*, originally spelled with such forms as *wer*, *weer* and *wear*. An *i* appears in the 16th century, and stays.

Either and *neither* are two more exceptions. The *i* seems to have replaced a *y*, which earlier had replaced an Old English yogh (Chapter 11). The pronunciation of these words varies today: some people say 'ee-ther' and some say 'eye-ther' (as in the Gershwins' song, 'Let's call the whole thing off'), and this variation goes back centuries. The *ei* spelling was a good representation of the 'ee' pronunciation, given its frequent use in other /i:/ words at the time. *Ai* was also a common Middle English spelling, presumably reflecting an 'eye' pronunciation, but as *ai* and *ei* were often used as alternative spellings (as Mulcaster noted), *ei* would certainly have come out on top. An additional push would again have come from Scotland, where the *ei* spellings were preferred in any case.

Heifer – *heahfore* in Old English (a 'high-goer', though why this should apply to heifers isn't at all obvious) – had a variety of spellings in Middle English, one of which was *ei*. It seems to have been the influence of the Bible that led to its popularity, in which it appears several times. It was *heyffer* in the translations by William Tyndale and the Bishops' Bible, and *heifer* in the Geneva and Douai-Rheims versions. Once the King James translators settled on it, its future was assured.

What about *eight*, along with *eighty*, *eighteenth*, etc.? It's an important Old English word, as all numerals are, appearing in such spellings as *ahta* and *eahta*. The Middle English equivalents included *eyʒte*, and the letter yogh was replaced by *gh* in due course (as we saw in Chapter 11). Here, too, Bible translations probably hastened its acceptance. It is spelled *eight* in Coverdale's translation (1535), and soon became the norm.

The remaining *ei* words are all easy to explain. Many are the result of an *e* occurring before a suffix beginning with *i*, along the same lines as in the *ie* examples above. We find *atheism, atheist, deify, nucleic, cuneiform* and a few more. Prefixes ending in *e* before a word beginning with *i* are illustrated by *reinforce* and *pre-install*. In *albeit*, each of the letters is pronounced separately. Foreign spellings (and sometimes pronunciations) have been quietly introduced in such loanwords as *reveille*, *Eid* and *rottweiler*, as well as in such names as *Heidi* and *Rheims*.

The total number of *ei* spellings is small in everyday language. There are rather more in the vocabulary of science and technology, through such coinages as *narceine, codeine, buddleia, batoidei, clupeiformes* and *ploceidae*. But even here we are talking about only a few dozen words, compared with the hundreds where '*i before e*' is the norm.

So, it's not that the various *ie* and *ei* spellings don't have an explanation. They do. But the factors are too great to reduce to a simple rule. It would need qualifying and qualifying in ways such as those illustrated above. On the other hand, we don't need to go so far as to say that all the 'exceptions' in this chapter need to be learned by heart as individual items, as some educationists have suggested. This is what a 2009 UK government report, *Support for Spelling*, had to say (p. 106):

> The i before e except after c rule is not worth teaching. It applies only to words in which the ie or ei stands for a clear /ee/ sound and unless this is known, words such as *sufficient*, *veil* and *their* look like exceptions. There are so few words where the ei spelling for the /ee/ sound follows the letter c that it is easier to learn the specific words: *receive*, *conceive*, *deceive* (+ the related words *receipt*, *conceit*, *deceit*), *perceive* and *ceiling*.

If the exceptions were as few as these, that recommendation would be fine. But there are rather more than is suggested, as this chapter illustrates. Is the only alternative to learn each one by heart? There is a middle road, as this chapter suggests, which a basic knowledge of grammar and word-history can provide.

For many in the late 18th century, the solution was much simpler. All we needed, they thought, was a good spelling model to follow.

Mrs Malaprop on reading and spelling

[Lydia has refused to give up the man she loves, much to the disgust of her guardian, Mrs Malaprop, and Sir Anthony Absolute, a wealthy baronet, who has other plans. She is told to go to her room.]

Mrs Malaprop: There's a little intricate hussy for you!

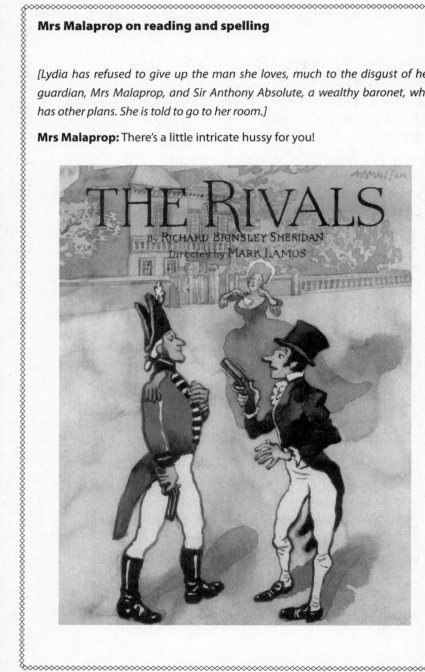

Sir Anthony: It is not to be wondered at, ma'am,— all this is the natural consequence of teaching girls to read. Had I a thousand daughters, by Heaven! I'd as soon have them taught the black art as their alphabet!

Mrs Malaprop: Nay, nay, Sir Anthony, you are an absolute misanthropy.

Sir Anthony: In my way hither, Mrs Malaprop, I observed your niece's maid coming forth from a circulating library! —She had a book in each hand— they were half-bound volumes, with marble covers!— From that moment I guessed how full of duty I should see her mistress!

Mrs Malaprop: Those are vile places, indeed!

Sir Anthony: Madam, a circulating library in a town is as an evergreen tree of diabolical knowledge! It blossoms through the year! — And depend on it, Mrs Malaprop, that they who are so fond of handling the leaves, will long for the fruit at last.

Mrs Malaprop: Fy, fy, Sir Anthony! you surely speak laconically.

Sir Anthony: Why, Mrs Malaprop, in moderation now, what would you have a woman know?

Mrs Malaprop: Observe me, Sir Anthony. I would by no means wish a daughter of mine to be a progeny of learning; I don't think so much learning becomes a young woman; for instance, I would never let her meddle with Greek, or Hebrew, or algebra, or simony, or fluxions, or paradoxes, or such inflammatory branches of learning—neither would it be necessary for her to handle any of your mathematical, astronomical, diabolical instruments.—But, Sir Anthony, I would send her, at nine years old, to a boarding-school, in order to learn a little ingenuity and artifice. Then, sir, she should have a supercilious knowledge in accounts;—and as she grew up, I would have her instructed in geometry, that she might know something of the contagious countries;—but above all, Sir Anthony, she should be mistress of orthodoxy, that she might not mis-spell, and mis-pronounce words so shamefully as girls usually do; and likewise that she might reprehend the true meaning of what she is saying. This, Sir Anthony, is what I would have a woman know;—and I don't think there is a superstitious article in it.

(From Richard Sheridan, *The Rivals*, 1775, I.ii)

25

The role of personalities

Many features of English spelling have been shaped because they were recommended by individual writers. Dr Johnson had the most influence on the way spelling evolved in Britain, even though some of the spellings he advocated have since been changed.

An interesting feature of Lindley Murray's chapter on 'Words in general, and the rules for spelling them' (Chapter 24) is the way he ends it. He seems to sense that the rules approach isn't the answer. In his final paragraph he acknowledges that English spelling isn't easy: 'The orthography of a great number of English words is far from being uniform, even amongst writers of distinction.' After giving some illustrations (such as *honour* and *honor*, *negotiate* and *negociate*), he observes: 'Some authority for deciding differences of this nature appears to be necessary.' But who should that authority be? Murray is in no doubt: 'where can we find one of equal pretensions with Dr Johnson's Dictionary?' This dictionary, he claims, 'has nearly fixed the external form of our language', and he finds this so valuable that 'it is earnestly to be hoped, that no author will henceforth, on slight grounds, be tempted to innovate'.

As so often with prescriptive writers, what they say at one point they contradict at another. When we look at the rules explaining how we use the letter *c*, we find this (p. 22):

> C, says Dr. Johnson, according to English
> orthography, never ends a word; and therefore we
> find in our best dictionaries, stick, block, publick,
> politick, etc. But many writers of later years omit
> the *k* in words of two or more syllables; and this
> practice is gaining ground, though it is productive
> of irregularities; such as writing mimic and
> mimickry; traffic and trafficking.

That is what Murray does himself – spelling *pathetic*, for example, whereas Johnson has *pathetick*.

Nonetheless, Murray is right in one respect: Johnson did 'fix' spelling to an appreciable extent. And people were prepared to use him as a model and follow his decisions. The statesman Lord Chesterfield, in a letter to the periodical *The World* in 1754, went almost over the top, referring to Johnson as the best person to fill the role of a language 'dictator':

> I give my vote for Mr Johnson to fill that great and
> arduous post. And I hereby declare that I make
> a total surrender of all my rights and privileges
> in the English language, as a freeborn British
> subject, to the said Mr Johnson, during the term
> of his dictatorship. Nay more; I will not only obey
> him, like an old Roman, as my dictator, but, like a

modern Roman, I will implicitly believe in him as my pope, and hold him to be infallible while in the chair; but no longer.

This is strong – and influential – stuff. Chesterfield's opinion was universally shared in Britain. During the 19th century, a copy of Johnson's *Dictionary* could be found in every educated person's library.

Johnson wasn't a great spelling innovator. He was well aware that many English spellings were so established that it would be pointless to try to change them, and he concludes in his Preface:

> I have often been obliged to sacrifice uniformity to custom; thus I write, in compliance with a numberless majority, *convey* and *inveigh*, *deceit* and *receipt*, *fancy* and *phantom*.

However, simply by including these versions, he in effect authorised them. And he gave a blessing to the latest additions to the alphabet:

> Our letters are commonly reckoned twenty-four, because anciently *i* and *j*, as well as *u* and *v*, were expressed by the same character; but as those letters, which had always different powers, have now different forms, our alphabet may be properly said to consist of twenty-six letters.

He nonetheless followed tradition in his *Dictionary* by conflating *i* / *j* and *u* / *v*, so that we see *inwreathe* immediately followed by *job*, and *vizier* followed by *ulcer*. But this practice eventually died out, and during the 1820s dictionaries began to show their modern twenty-six-letter format.

Johnson's influence is also apparent in the way he handles usage variations. Here he always refers to the source language. He writes, about words which are 'variantly written', that he will make a decision based on 'their original languages':

> thus I write *enchant, enchantment, enchanter,* after the *French,* and *incantation* after the *Latin;* thus *entire* is chosen rather than *intire,* because it passed to us not from the *Latin integer,* but from the *French entier.*

If there's a choice, he goes for the Latin: thus we find him spelling *inquire,* not *enquire* (Latin *inquiro,* French *enquirer*). Etymology rules again.

Several of our modern spelling practices stem from the decisions Johnson made. *Practice* is a case in point. He distinguishes *practice* as a noun from *practise* as a verb. It was one of several *c/s* decisions which also exercised the minds of the French scribes (Chapter 12): he affirms *prophecy* and *prophesy, council* and *counsel,* and, following the pattern of nouns taking a *c,* opts for *pretence* and *defence.* On the other hand, he isn't entirely consistent: we see *license* for both the noun and the verb, despite giving French *licencer* as its source. And he decided to distinguish *humour* and *humorous* on etymological grounds, though the sources are unclear. Noah Webster would later notice these anomalies and make a different set of decisions for American English (Chapter 26). British usage is not always comfortable with it: the *Oxford English Dictionary*, for example, recognises both *humorist* and *humourist*, *humourless* and *humorless*.

Another example is Johnson's distinction between *travel* and *travail*. This is quite deliberate, as we see from the note he adds at the beginning of his entry on *travel*:

> This word is generally supposed originally the same with *travail*, and to differ only as particular from general; in some writers the word is written alike in all its senses; but it is more convenient to write *travail* for *labour*, and *travel* for *journey*.

So that's what we do today. But notice that the reason for our modern practice stems from nothing more than an opinion – 'it is more convenient'.

Something else has happened to *travail* since that decision was made. It has developed an alternative pronunciation. Perhaps some people still pronounce *travail* as they do *travel*, but most now make the second syllable rhyme with *ale*. It's an example of 'spelling pronunciation', where the way a word is spoken is made to conform to how it is spelled. It is a practice Johnson wholeheartedly approved of:

> For pronunciation the best general rule is, to consider those as the most elegant speakers who deviate least from the written words.

And so, today, we find many who pronounce the first *i* in *medicine*, the *h* in *nihilism* and *philharmonic*, the *p* in *empty*, the *w* in *towards* and the *t* in *ostler* and *often*.

Henry Fowler thought this was a terrible practice, as he says in his entry on *often*:

> The sounding of the *t* ... is practised by two oddly consorted classes – the academic speakers who affect a more precise enunciation than their neighbours ... & the uneasy half-literates who like to prove that they can spell.

Ouch! But some spelling-pronunciations have become standard, despite Fowler's opposition, such as *conduit* for earlier 'condit', *waistcoat* for earlier 'weskit', and *forehead* alongside earlier 'forrid' (remembered especially for its rhyme with *horrid* in the nursery tale of the little girl who had a little curl). *Herb* (and its related forms, such as *herbal*) has gone both ways: originally *erbe*, there was never an /h/ in the pronunciation; but once the *h* arrived in the spelling (another example of Latin influence, *herba*) things changed. It began to be pronounced in the 19th century in Britain; but remained silent in the USA.

Sometimes Johnson backs the wrong horse, as in the case mentioned above of *c* never ending an English word. He was thinking not only of words like *black* and *stick*, which had had a *ck* spelling for centuries (Chapter 7), but words with more than one syllable, such as *musick*, *critick* and *acrostick*. Nobody quite knew how to spell such words. *Music*, for example, had been written in over forty different ways by the 18th century, such as *musique*, *musik*, *musicck*, *musicke* and *musickque*, in which *k*, *c* and *q* were used in every

conceivable combination. Johnson saw that choosing *ck* would be a benefit, as all words ending in the
sound /ɪk/ would be spelled in the same way. But it
was the wrong decision. Many people were already
using such spellings as *music*, and when Noah
Webster opted to get rid of the *k*, its fate was sealed.
We see it today only in elegant archaisms, as when
performers of early music spell their name as *Musick*.

Many of Johnson's words show the distance that
English spelling had to travel before it reached the
present-day standard, such as his use of *fewel*, *rain-
deer* and *villany*. He doesn't distinguish between
flower and *flour*: both are spelled *flower*. Some words
were printed solid which today would be given
spaces, as with *anotherguess*, *brownstudy*, *illnature*,
welldone, *wellmet*, *whitewine*. The choice between final
-l and *-ll* was still in flux: we see *downfal* and *petrol*
but *pitfall* and *comptroll*. So was the choice between
-or and *-our*: *confessor* and *inheritor* alongside *oratour*
and *possessour*. Johnson often comments on the variation. He acknowledges that there are problems with
certain endings: *resistance* or *resistence*, *sailer* or *sailor*.
And he points out in the Preface:

> Some combinations of letters having the same
> power are used indifferently without any
> discoverable reason of choice, as in *choak*, *choke*;
> *soap*, *sope*; *fewel*, *fuel*, and many others; which I have
> sometimes inserted twice, that those who search
> for them under either form, may not search in vain.

Other examples are *shrug* and *shrugg*, *choir* and *quire*, *summersault* and *somersault, evesdropper* and *eavesdropper*, and *hearse* and *herse.*

The 19th-century printers did a lot of mopping up, for none of these examples are variants today. But just as one set of variants began to disappear, another set arose, thanks to what was happening in America.

26

Another personality

What Johnson did for British English, Webster did for American English. Americans eventually adopted most of his recommendations for forming an orthographically distinctive 'new nation', though not all of his proposals found favour.

It's a commonplace today that British and American spelling differs. British readers notice *catalog* and *defense* and *traveling*. American readers notice *catalogue* and *defence* and *travelling*. The differences are sometimes very prominent. Terry Pratchett's 1983 novel is either *The Colour of Magic* or *The Color of Magic*, depending on where you live. And American usage is changing traditional British practice, so the issue is a real one, affecting daily decisions in British English about how to spell certain words. Is it *archeology* or *archaeology*, *meter* or *metre*? There are two orthographies for Standard English in the world now. How did this situation come about?

It is largely due to one man, Noah Webster. Working as a schoolteacher in Connecticut during the American Revolution, he was struck by the poor quality of traditional teaching materials, and especially by their failure to reflect the ethos and environment of the 'new nation'. In 1783 he published a textbook which would become the standard introduction for generations of young American readers: *The American Spelling Book*, often called (from its cover) 'the blue-backed speller'.

The year of publication is significant. It was the same year that the American War of Independence ended. In 1789 Webster would go on to publish a dissertation advocating the development of an American standard of English. It was a matter of honour, he asserted, 'as an independent nation ... to have a system of our own, in language as well as government'. Spelling reform would be a major part of this: 'a difference between the English orthography and the American ... is an object of vast political consequence.'

As the spelling book went through its early editions, we can see the new approach emerging. He acknowledges the British tradition – notably Johnson – in the Preface to his speller, and writes:

> As the orthography of our language is not yet settled with precision, I have in this particular generally followed the most approved authors of the last and present century.

But by 1800, although British influence is still there, it's clearly on the wane. He has dropped the final *k* in words like *music* and *critic*, and begun to replace *-our* by *-or*. Not all words are yet spelled with *-or*:

alongside *endeavor, favor, flavor, humor, labor, honor, neighbor* and *favorite* we still see *behaviour, rigour* and *parlour*. But by 1828, when he published his major work, *An American Dictionary of the English Language*, we find all these words spelled with *-or*. And that dictionary includes many other words that have since come to define the features of American English spelling – *e* for *ae* (as in *cesarian* and *archeology*), *er* for *re* (as in *center* and *fiber*), *se* for *ce* (as in *defense* and *license*), *l* for *ll* (as in *marvelous* and *traveler*), and *ll* for *l* (as in *appall* and *instill*). We see new individual spellings too, such as *ax* (British *axe*), *caldron* (*cauldron*), *diarrhea* (*diarrhoea*), *maneuver* (*manoeuvre*), *mustaches* (*moustaches*), *wagon* (*waggon*) and *story* (*storey*).

Not all the spellings that would eventually identify American English were in place in 1828. Webster still uses *gue* in such words as *catalogue, dialogue* and *monologue*, and it would take some time before the *-g* spelling would replace it. His *Dictionary* still shows *practice, dough-nut, draughtsman, sceptical* and *theatre*. Variants are still being given: *chequer* is cross-referred to *checker, connexion* to *connection, enquire* to *inquire, ensure* to *insure, foetus* to *fetus, grey* to *gray, inflexion* to *inflection, oesophagus* to *esophagus, plough* to *plow*. At times, such as when we see *center* as well as *theatre*, we can sense him being pulled in two directions, and sometimes there are parallel entries: he has entries for both *feces* and *faeces, gaol* and *jail, gage* and *gauge*. At other times he is in no doubt: *mould*, see *mold*, he writes, adding 'an incorrect orthography'.

Webster had far more influence on spelling, as an innovator, than Johnson; but not all of Webster's innovations survived. He recommended *fether* and *tung*, for example, but *feather* and *tongue* prevailed. And if we look at his list of 'absurd' spellings in the Preface to his speller, we can see that some were accepted, some survived with modifications, and some were ignored:

> The spelling of such words as *publick, favour, neighbour, bead, prove, phlegm, his, give, debt, rough, well* instead of the more natural and easy method, *public, favor, nabor, bed, proov, flem, hiz, giv, det, ruf, wel*, has the plea of antiquity in its favour; and yet I am convinced that common sense and convenience will sooner or later get the better of the present absurd practice.

There were later changes in several other words: for example, *musquetoe* in the speller became *musketoe* in the *Dictionary*, but both are still some way from *mosquito*.

Meanwhile, back on the British ranch, there was fury at the American changes. 'Look,' says Henry Alford, Dean of Canterbury, in his bestselling book *A Plea for the Queen's English* (1863), 'at the process of deterioration which our Queen's English has undergone at the hands of the Americans', and his first illustrations are from spelling (p. 10):

> The first remark that I have to make shall be on the trick now so universal across the Atlantic and

becoming in some quarters common among us in England, of leaving out the 'u' in the termination 'our'... Now the objection to this is, not that it makes very ugly words, totally unlike anything in the English language before (for we do thus spell some of the words thus derived, for example, *author, governor, emperor*, &c.), but that it is part of a movement to reduce our spelling to uniform rule as opposed to usage, and to help forward the obliteration of all trace of the derivation and history of words.

He quotes with approval 'the late Archbishop Hare', who had expressed the hope that 'such abominations as *honor* and *favor* would henceforth be confined to the cards of the great vulgar'. His hope would not be fulfilled.

Webster was an American patriot, but he was in addition a perceptive critic and a practical teacher. One of his comments in the Preface to his speller remains just as valid today:

Among the defects and absurdities found in the books of this kind hitherto used, we may rank the want of a thorough investigation of the sounds in the English language, and the powers of the several letters.

What do the French say? *Plus ça change* ... The more things change, the more they remain the same.

27

Printers and publishers

Far from introducing consistency, the growth in the number of dictionaries during the 19th century resulted in many conflicting recommendations about spelling. Publishers and printers evolved their own practices, and introduced their own house styles – but these didn't always agree either.

Where Samuel Johnson and Noah Webster went, others were quick to follow. No one could really compete with their hugely successful publications, but that didn't stop others trying. It's a bit of a cliché to talk about a century as being an 'age of' something, but the 19th century could certainly lay claim to being called the 'age of dictionaries'.

The first half of the 19th century was remarkable for the number of dictionaries that were published on both sides of the Atlantic. Joseph Worcester provides a catalogue at the beginning of his own *Dictionary of the English Language* (1859), and identifies sixty-four other works published in England since Johnson and thirty in America since Webster – almost one a year. These were all general dictionaries, on English as a whole. In addition, the period saw the publication of over 200 specialised dictionaries and glossaries, as well as thirty encyclopaedias, showing how compilers were under pressure to keep up with the increase in knowledge and terminology taking place in all aspects of science and technology – not least arising out of the Industrial Revolution. If you wanted a dictionary of sea terms, or of architecture, or of medicine, by 1850 you had plenty of choice.

As an example of the level of detail of these works, take the revision in 1805 by John William Norrie – a 'teacher of navigation', as he is described on the title page – of a marine dictionary by William Falconer, first published in 1769. This is the full title page description:

> Falconer improved and modernised. The mariner's new and complete Naval Dictionary, in two parts: Part I Being a copius vocabulary of the British marine containing a copius explanation of the technical terms and sea phrases employed in the construction, equipment, furniture, machinery, movements, management, and military as well as naval operations of a ship; together with a full account of every thing relating to masts, sails, yards, rigging, &c. &c. Illustrated with thirteen engravings. Part II A modern French marine dictionary; containing all the sea phrases and technical terms used in the Marine of the French Republic, and the same faithfully translated into the English language. The whole including all the modern improvements and alterations in the British and French naval tactics, &c.

It ran to 484 pages, not by any means the largest of the dictionaries on this subject published at the time.

Nor were dictionaries the only linguistic products. Other aspects of language were being presented to a public anxious to improve their abilities in grammar, pronunciation, punctuation and spelling. The attitudes expressed by Lord Chesterfield and Dean Alford were now being taught in schools and permeated society – not only in Britain and the USA, but also in Australia, New Zealand, India, South Africa and other parts of the British Empire. Publishers competed to make books on grammar, punctuation and spelling colourful and appealing, especially to children.

For spelling, it was the age of alliterative and rhyming texts. Letter recognition was taught through personalities – Angry Alice, Sorrowful Simon, Timid Tabitha – who rhymed their way through life.

> *The crying Simon here you view.*
> *I hope he's not like me, or you.*

Simon and the others often got into scrapes which just happened to illustrate the frequent use of their letter. It's an approach still widely used today, in such series as Lyn Wendon's *Letterland*, and books like Eric Carle's *All About Arthur (An Absolutely Absurd Ape)* or the *Horrid Henry* tales. Arthur, for example, meets several new friends under letter *L*:

> In Louisville he met Leo, a lonely lion licking a

lollipop; Lana, a lovely llama; and Lisa, a little lady lizard.

Letter recognition is a critical stage in the process of learning to read, but an initial-letter approach doesn't help acclimatise children to spelling, because it ignores the fact that letters don't appear with equal frequency at the beginning of words. It presents an unreal view of the writing system, as is notoriously illustrated by *X*. Alphabet-book writers have always had trouble with this one, having to resort to arcane and age-unrelated examples, such as *xylophone*, *xebec*, *X-ray* and *Xenophon* (this last from an 1815 book called *The Paragon of Alphabets*). Charles Dickens made some caustic remarks about it (p. 120). The whole issue would have been avoided if, instead of the mantra 'A is for —', it had been 'A is in —'. 'X is in fox' presents no difficulty. But that solution was never adopted.

Correctness was everything in the 19th century, and that meant consistency. Two social factors made this a priority. First, there was a huge increase in the amount of material being written and read – novels, essays, Bibles, newspapers, broadsheets, advertisements, magazines, penny dreadfuls, maps and all kinds of ephemera (tickets, posters, street signs, catalogues, business cards, letterheads, etc.). New methods of printing (such as the rotary press in 1843) and distribution made all this material accessible to the population, through bookshops, libraries (public, private and circulating) and the postal service.

At the same time, the 19th century saw a huge increase in the number of people able to read and write. Estimates vary, depending on how the notion of literacy is measured, but the likely growth in Britain during the century was from around half the population to over 90 per cent. And we mustn't forget that the population itself was rapidly increasing – in Britain from around 10 million in 1801 to nearly 40 million in 1901. The growth in the USA was even more dramatic, from around 5 million in 1800 to 76 million a century later.

All this meant a new role for publishers and printers. Ultimately, these were the people who were effectively 'in charge' of the writing system. The publishing business was becoming increasingly professional. Not only were there more publishing houses, there were more printers, and they were becoming powerful. In the USA, the National Typographical Union was founded in 1852 and the Government Printing Office in 1861. In Britain, the London Association of Correctors of the Press was formed in 1854. It was known dismissively as the 'comma club' – an unfair appellation, because their role (as those of copy-editors today) involved far more than checking on punctuation and spelling. But orthography was certainly part of their remit. Their job was to ensure consistency and maintain standards.

But where were these standards to come from? Sporadic initiatives to establish an academy, along the lines of the French Academy, had come to nothing, as Dr Johnson had predicted they would. In any case, it would be impossible for such an institution to hold sway over a language that was being used in so many countries, and which was developing different regional standards. The printing industry had no alternative but to rely on the major dictionaries. But they were immediately faced with a problem. These dictionaries offered alternative forms, and often disagreed among themselves. Joseph Worcester, whose *Dictionary of the English Language* (1859) sold widely on both sides of the Atlantic, even included a list of 'words of doubtful or various orthography'. There are over 1,700 of them, such as *villanous* vs. *villainous, toilet* vs. *toilette, show* vs. *shew, judgment* vs. *judgement, czar* vs. *tzar* and *tsar*. Worcester recommends the former alternative in these cases, but not always with any great conviction: 'In some cases, words are so variously affected by etymology, analogy, and general usage, that it is difficult to determine what orthography is best supported.' Other lexicographers were similarly hesitant.

This didn't help the printers one bit. Faced with alternative spellings, they had no choice but to make a decision for themselves, as William Caxton had done 400 years before. They came up with their own solution: to make the principle of consistency a priority, and to develop their own house style. In Britain, Horace Hart, a member of the London Association of Correctors of the Press, began collecting material in the 1860s, which eventually formed the basis of a style guide for Oxford University Press. First issued in 1893, it became known as *Hart's Rules*, and proved to be a highly influential manual. In the USA, the Government Printing Office issued its style guide in 1887. The *Chicago Manual of Style* appeared in 1906. And so, slowly but surely, we reach the situation we see today, where each publisher has its own house style.

Do they all agree? Of course not. Decisions were made by individuals, often based on little more than personal taste and a vague sense of 'it's always been that way'. Thus we find in the UK today one style guide (e.g. *The Times*) recommending *moveable* and another (e.g. *The Guardian* and *Observer*) recommending *movable*. Both newspapers opt for *judgment*; but the style guides of Oxford and Cambridge University Presses make a first choice of *judgement*. OUP and CUP don't always agree either. And style preferences can change even within one institution: for example, *The Times* used -*ize* endings until the 1990s, when it changed to -*ise*. Today its style guide says 'avoid the z construction in almost all cases'. But the editors of the *Oxford English Dictionary*, as we saw in Chapter 14, state firmly: 'in this Dictionary the termination is uniformly written -*ize*'.

In America, where individual rights are especially respected, we see special cases upsetting any notion of total consistency. In 1890 the Board of Geographic Names was founded to promote the consistent spelling of place names on maps and charts. It was sorely needed. French, Indian, Spanish and traditional English spellings were in competition. A state such as Wisconsin was being spelled in a variety of ways, such as *Wiskonsin*, *Wisconsan* and *Ouisconsin*. By the end of the century, over 7,000 names had had their spellings approved by the Board, and naming principles were established. Hyphens and accents were out. So were silent letters: places ending in *-burgh* were to call themselves *-burg*, those in *-borough* would become *-boro*. But, as we saw in Chapter 19, this didn't please the good citizens of Pittsburgh, Pennsylvania, which remains an exception to this day.

So there we have it – two major British institutions going in opposite directions, and individuals in the USA insisting on being an exception to the rules. William Caxton's comment is as relevant as ever (Chapter 18): 'Lo! What should a man in these days now write?'

Spelling wars

[*The residents of an American boarding-house debate spelling at breakfast, as reported by Oliver Wendell Holmes. A young man from Boston launches a ferocious attack on the practices adopted in Webster's unabridged dictionary, and shows just how emotional the subject had become.*]

Mr Webster couldn't spell, sir, or wouldn't spell, sir – at any rate, he didn't spell; and the end of it was a fight between the owners of some copyrights and the dignity of this noble language which we have inherited from our English fathers.

Language! – the blood of the soul, sir! into which our thoughts run and out of which they grow! We know what a word is worth here in Boston. Young Sam Adams got up on the stage at Commencement, out at Cambridge there, with his gown on, the Governor and Council looking on in the name of his Majesty, King George the Second, and the girls looking down out of the galleries, and taught people how to spell a word that wasn't in the Colonial dictionaries! *R-e, re, s-i-s, sis, t-a-n-c-e, tance, Resistance!* That was in '43, and it was a good many years before the Boston boys began spelling it with their muskets; but when they did begin, they spelt it so loud that the old bedridden women in the English almshouses heard every syllable! Yes, yes, yes, it was a good while before those other two Boston boys got the class so far along that it could spell those two hard words, *Independence* and *Union*!

I tell you what, sir, there are a thousand lives, aye, sometimes a million, go to get a new word into a language that is worth speaking. We know what language means too well here in Boston to play tricks with it.

(From *The Professor at the Breakfast-Table*, 1859, Ch. 1)

28

Changing practices

Despite the evolution of Standard English, there is a huge amount of spelling variation in contemporary writing. Several factors account for the variants.

Just how much variation is there in Modern English spelling? It is 150 years since Joseph Worcester and the other lexicographers worried about it. We might expect most of it to have been eliminated by now. In fact, the opposite seems to have happened. There is more variation in spelling today than ever before.

In 1986, English grammarian Sidney Greenbaum carried out a survey of words with alternative spellings in a general-purpose desk dictionary. He took letter A as a sample, and found an average of three variant forms per page, as illustrated by these examples from the beginning of letter A:

abetter	abettor	acclimatise	acclimatize
abridgable	abridgeable	acouchi	acouchy
absinthe	absinth	adieus	adieux
abulia	aboulia	adrenalin	adrenaline
accessory	accessary	aegis	egis

There were cases of three variants (such as *aerie*,

aery, erie) and even four (*anaesthetise, anaesthetize, anesthetise, anesthetize*). The variants amounted to 5.8 per cent of all the A words. I've carried out the same exercise on some of the other letters of the alphabet, and the percentage is similar. However, a desk dictionary includes only a small proportion of the words in English – perhaps 150,000 out of the million or so that comprise the total English lexicon. The amount of variation in a scientific or technical dictionary is going to be much greater, because of the frequency of words using a suffix such as *-in/ -ine* or a prefix such as *paedo-/pedo-* or *archae-/arche-*. A similar sampling from specialised dictionaries shows a variation level of around 14 per cent.

The increase is partly due to differences between American and British English, with American usage increasingly influencing British, but it also reflects different intuitions over which of two spellings better reflects the content of the specialism. For example, we are more likely to find the conservative *ae* spelling in relation to subjects which have historical content. In a Google search in 2011, the 'modern' subject of *pediatrics* was ten times more frequent than *paediatrics* and *etiology* was five times more frequent than *aetiology*; but the 'historical' subject of *archaeology* was four times more frequent than *archeology*, and there was little to choose in frequency between words beginning with *palaeo-* or *paleo-*. Academic tradition is also an important factor. The term *aesthetics* is normal in the context of art, but it is *esthetics* in the context of dentistry. And there may be mixed usage: a journal or company may retain one spelling in its title while using the alternative in its pages. The *Atlanta Institute of Aesthetics*, for example, is (as the home page of its website explains) 'a premier skin care school with a commitment to teach esthetics from a modern, holistic perspective'.

Different cultural traditions can also motivate individual spellings and thus contribute to variation. Spelling does not exist only to communicate words intelligibly; it helps to convey identity. If informed people write *nocturn*, they are talking about something religious; if they write *nocturne*, they are into music or the arts. Any group of musicians using *Musick* in their name must be showing a commitment to an early English repertoire (Chapter 25). And if we see a sudden increase in the use of *x*, *y* and *z* in brand-names, we are probably in a pharmacy: *Zovirax, Prozac, Zadaxin, Xanax, Zyban, Xylocaine* ...

An old spelling can help show the character of a variety of English, such as legal language (*shew* for *showed*, *serjeant* for *sergeant*) or religious language (*alway* for *always*, *encrease* for *increase*). And a specific tradition can motivate exceptional spellings. *Crucifixion* is a good example of a word which has retained a spelling in a religious setting which, when compared with other uses of this word-ending, is impossible (*detection*, never *detexion*) or archaic (*connexion*): it ought to be *crucifiction* (compare *fiction*), but the influence of Latin (*crucifixus*) introduced the *x* for *crucifix* in the 15th century and it became the norm in Christianity. Cultural preferences may also motivate the use of a particular spelling, such as to show a political or religious identity (*Québec* vs. *Quebec*, *Muslim* vs. *Moslem*).

The percentage of spelling variation rises again if we include in our notion of spelling other phenomena than the selection and ordering of letters. There are many variations in capitalisation, for example: is it *moon* or *Moon*, *bible* or *Bible*, *president* or *President*, *prime minister* or *Prime Minister*? There are variations in spacing and hyphenation: is it *flower pot, flower-pot* or *flowerpot*? *No one, no-one* or *noone*? There are variations in the use of the apostrophe: is it *Kings Cross* or *King's Cross* (for the area in London), *1980s* or *1980's*? If we include all these, the variation level rises to over 20 per cent. And if we add the transliteration of proper names from other languages to our list, it rises still further. Is it *Tschaikovsky, Tchaikovsky, Tschaikofsky, Tchaikofsky*? *Tutankhamen, Tutankhamun, Tut'ankhamun*? *Ibn al-Khatib, Ibn-Al-Khatib, Abenaljatib, Ben al-Hatib*? Individual publishers have to make up their minds which variant to use and stay with it, but when we look at the language as a whole, we see many competing choices. They are a real headache for copy-editors and indexers.

The problem is partly one of language change. The punctuation of words can vary as time goes by. As *e-mail* became more widespread, people began writing it as *email*. *Chat-rooms* became *chatrooms*.

Around 16,000 words lost their hyphen in the sixth edition of the *Shorter Oxford Dictionary*, published in 2007, causing both delight (among those who were never sure whether to use a hyphen or not) and dismay (among those who did). In that dictionary, some of the previously hyphenated words were shown solid (such as *leapfrog* and *touchline*); others were shown spaced (such as *ice cream* and *test tube*). This is all part of a modern trend to omit word punctuation: graphic designers often say it adds undesirable 'clutter' to the appearance of a word. Thus, as well as the omission of hyphens, the 20th century saw the gradual removal of full-stops in abbreviations (*BBC* for *B.B.C.*, *Mr* for *Mr.*) and apostrophes were left out of place names and signs (*Harrods* for *Harrod's*, *Waterstones* for *Waterstone's*, *womens* for *women's* in the clothing department of a big store). There is no unanimity, of course. Different dictionaries, stores and designers make different decisions. Over time a consensus can evolve, but new sources of variation are never far away – such as we see currently in the impact of the Internet.

Roger McGough on spelling

twould be nice to be
an apostrophe
floating above an s
hovering like a paper kite
in between the its
eavesdropping, tiptoeing
high above the thats
an inky comet
spiralling
the highest tossed of hats

('Apostrophe', 1976)

Is a bad speller
one
who casts a wicked spell?

(From *Lucky*, 1993)

Never have an operation you cannot spell
Or live in a town you mispronounce.

('Bath – Avon', in *Defying Gravity*, 1992)

29
The Internet

A new source of spelling variation is the Internet. The future role of the electronic medium in influencing spelling is unclear, but it is likely that a simplification of the most irregular spellings will be one of the outcomes.

The Internet is in its early days, so its influence on English spelling has hitherto been very limited. Some of its services (chat, texting, Twitter, social networking) have popularised some old abbreviations (such as *c* for *see*, *u* for *you*, *2* for *to*) and introduced a few new ones (such as *lol*), but these are largely restricted to the technology context in which they arose, and are only occasionally encountered in the wider orthographic world. Novelties, whose long-term effect on the language remains to be seen, include minimalist or zero capitalisation in messages (no sentence-initial capital, the use of *i* for the pronoun *I*), the use of repeated letters (*I'm sooooooo happy*), and the replacement of normal letters by other symbols, as seen in *@command*, *Micro$oft*, *AO£* ('AOL'), *d00dz* ('dudes'), and *c%%l* ('cool'). We are used to apostrophes in names (*O'Malley*) but not usually exclamation marks (*Yahoo!*).

Several coinages provide a new look to English spelling, especially with names. We have never seen anything before quite like the use of a lower-case initial for a brand-name, as in *iPod, iPhone, iSense* and *eBay*, or airline companies such as *easyJet* and *jetBlue*, and it is not yet clear how to handle them, especially when we want one of these words to begin a sentence. There are precedents for introducing a capital in the middle of a word (as in such names as *McDonald's* and chemical substances such as *CaSi*, calcium silicate), but brand-names have hugely increased its everyday visibility, as seen in *AltaVista, AskJeeves, PlayStation, YouTube* and *MasterCard*. Even three caps can be found, as in *QuarkXPress*. The phenomenon is referred to in various ways, such as bicaps (bicapitalisation), intercaps, incaps, medial caps and midcaps, as well as more picturesque names such as Camel-Case (the capitals form the humps) and BumpyCase. The trend is by no means restricted to the Internet, as seen in the names of publishers (*HarperCollins*), film companies (*DreamWorks*), TV series (*East-Enders*), and TV characters (the redoubtable *Sponge-Bob SquarePants*).

It is indeed early days, but it is likely that variation will increase as the Internet evolves. One factor will be the need to find novel domain names. All the common words in English, in their normal spelling, have now been used as URLs (uniform resource locators) to identify websites, so anyone wishing to add a new file to what is available must now devise an address that is different. This is usually done by stringing words together (as in *www.shakespeareswords. com*), but the longer the string the more risk there is of typing error. The alternative is to explore the use of shorter words with non-standard spellings, as long as the deviant form is easy to remember. We can already find several domain names using *txt* instead of *text* (*txttools, txtloan, txtcash,* etc.) and replacing a plural *-s* ending with a *-z* (*tunez, filmz, moviez, filez,* etc.). These are likely to increase.

The other possible cause of more online spelling variation is the unconscious desire for simplified spelling. This has been a recurrent theme in the history of English since the 16th century, and many schemes for spelling reform have been proposed. Every year I receive at least one new proposal from an enthusiastic reformer, sometimes worked out in meticulous detail. The problem, of course, is that every scheme is idiosyncratic, and has strengths and weaknesses. It simply isn't possible to find an agreed set of principles to simplify a thousand years of orthographic history, and even if it were, it wouldn't be possible to implement them all at once. It took time for the complexity of the present system to grow, and it will take time for it to diminish. The Internet, however, could hasten the process.

Spelling conventions, in the end, come down to majority usage. If enough people vote to use a new spelling, or object to one, then – as we saw in the case of Pittsburgh (Chapter 19) – change will take place.

On the Internet, what we see is people voting with their fingers. The contrast with traditional writing in the public domain is striking. With such outputs as blogging, chatrooms, and social networking sites, there are no copy-editors and proofreaders checking that traditional norms are being followed and, when they are not, introducing corrections. When I put a post up on my blog, I can spell, punctuate, coin words and use informal grammar as much as I want. Nobody is monitoring what I write to make sure it conforms to a publisher's house style (Chapter 30). I will be cautious over introducing change, of course. If I deviate too markedly from Standard English norms, my readers may not understand me. Some may be so distracted or irritated by the deviations that they fail to pay attention to my content – or even stop reading it altogether. But if enough people individually opt for a particular non-standard usage, eventually readers stop noticing it, and it becomes part of the standard language. That is how language change operates.

Spelling is by no means immune from such an outcome, and the words that are likely to be initially affected are the ones which cause us greatest difficulty. Spelling books often include a list of the commonest spelling errors in English, such as *ocurence*, *occurence*, *ocurrence* and other variants for *occurrence*; and similar uncertainty over doubled letters for such words as *millennium*, *accommodation* and *recommend* (the reason for this is discussed in Chapter 35). The title of Vivian Cook's 2004 anthology reflects the trend: *Accomodating Brocolli in the Cemetary: Or Why Can't Anybody Spell?* Only relatively recent convention stops us using *recomend*, for example, which is how this word was originally spelled when it arrived in English in the 1400s. And so it would not be surprising to find it increasing in frequency on the Internet, and eventually becoming a legitimate alternative to *recommend*, perhaps eventually ousting the latter altogether. In 2012 there were over a billion instances of *recommend* found in a Google search, but there were over 68 million instances of *recomend*. That is an amazing total. One generation's errors can be the next generation's norms.

Dictionary editors are reluctant to include spelling changes, well aware that they will attract strong criticism from those who see linguistic change as a regrettable lowering of standards. But if usage builds up, eventually they have to recognise that a change has taken place. As the BBC periodical *The Listener* put it in 1977, 'The mis-spelling of the quasi-scientific term *minuscule* as *miniscule* is now so common it is close to becoming accepted English.' Today we see *miniscule* listed in dictionaries on both sides of the Atlantic as simply a 'variant' of *minuscule*, though often with a health warning reflecting its contentious history.

Silent letters, especially those introduced by the 16th-century classicists (Chapter 21), are likely to be the first to go. I have been following the fate of the *h* in *rhubarb* in the Google database over the past few years. In 2006 there were just a few hundred instances of *rubarb*; in 2008 a few thousand; in 2010 there were 91,000; at the beginning of 2011 this had increased to 657,000, and by the end of the year it had passed a million. The ratios are the interesting thing: those 91,000 instances of *rubarb* in 2010 compared to 3,210,000 instances of *rhubarb* – a ratio of 1:35. The following year, 657,000 *rubarbs* compared to 13 million *rhubarbs* – a ratio of 1:20. And later that year *rubarb* passed the million mark. If it carries on like this, *rubarb* will overtake *rhubarb* as the commonest online spelling in the next five years. And where the online orthographic world goes in one decade, I suspect the offline world will go in the next.

So, variation is increasing – but we mustn't exaggerate the problem. If nearly a quarter of the words in English are variable, this means that over three-quarters are not. And most of the common words in the language display no variation at all. Standard spelling is a reality. The vast majority of the words I read in an American newspaper are spelled in exactly the same way as their equivalents in a British newspaper, and the same applies to English-language newspapers, magazines, books, websites and printed ephemera all over the world. But ironically, the fact that standard spelling exists is itself a factor in promoting variation of a different kind. Given a linguistic norm, people like to deviate from it, for all kinds of reasons.

Lower-case only

Don Marquis created archy, a cockroach who butts his head against the keys of a typewriter to write his poems, chiefly about his friend Mehitabel, an alley cat who was Queen Cleopatra in an earlier life. He is unable to reach the shift key, so everything comes out without capital letters or punctuation, as he explains ...

say comma boss comma capital
i apostrophe m getting tired of
being joshed about my
punctuation period capital t followed by
he idea seems to be
that capital i apostrophe m
ignorant where punctuation
is concerned period capital n followed by
o such thing semi
colon the fact is that
the mechanical exigencies of
the case prevent my use of
all the characters on the
typewriter keyboard period
capital i apostrophe m
doing the best capital
i can under difficulties semi colon
and capital i apostrophe m
grieved at the unkindness
of the criticisms period please
consider that my name
is signed in small
caps period
archy period

('archy protests', in 'archys life of mehitabel', 1934)

30

Showing identity

Spelling exists to express identity as well as to guarantee intelligibility, and the outcome is a large number of playful variations. We see them especially in commercial trade names, in the names of characters in children's stories, in the dialect spellings used in literature, and in many domestic settings.

In 1926, Louise Pound, an American college professor, wrote about 'The Kraze for "K"':

> there is no mistaking the kall of 'k' over our kountry, our kurious kontemporary kraving for it, and its konspicuous use in the klever koinages of kommerce.

She was thinking of such words as *Krazy, Kleen, Kwik, Karpet* and *Korner* when forming part of a trade name, as well as such spellings as *Kleenex* and *Tastykake*. The practice of replacing a *c* or *q* by *k* in this way can be traced back to at least the early 19th century, and goes well beyond trade names. For example, the origins of *OK* lie in *oll korrect* ('all correct'), first recorded in a Boston newspaper in 1839 as part of a vogue for humorous respellings. But it was the commercial world that turned a local humorous pastime into a major genre, with the names of products character-ised by a range of variant forms such as *hi* ('high'), *lo* ('low'), *nu* ('new'), *supa* ('super'), *U* ('you'), *R* ('are') and *eze* ('ease' or 'easy'), and the replacement of *-ight* in such words as *lite, nite, rite* and *brite*. Some of these non-standard forms have come to be used in informal writing outside of the commercial context, especially in American English. A few, such as *hi-fi* (never *high-fi*), have made the transition into print everywhere.

Trade names – like all proper names – are not really part of a language. I can be aware of the names of people, places and products in France without speaking a word of French. But names do exercise a linguistic influence, and especially upon spell-ing. Our intuitions about what is orthographically possible are shaped by our exposure to what we see around us in daily life. And it is in the area of proper names that we see some of the most impor-tant innovations in contemporary English spelling, adding to the variation that already exists in general vocabulary.

The reasons for adopting a non-standard spelling in a commercial name are usually pragmatic: to make a product stand out, to catch the eye, to be remem-bered, to make customers enjoy the joke. A difference in spelling suggests a difference in attitude, which (the company hopes) will transfer to the product in a positive way. That is why we see these spellings most often in trades which are trying to convey to their customers an approach which is special, innovative or fashionable. Hair salons, for example, go in for such spellings as *Cutts*, *Kuts* and *Kropps*, and often play with endings, as in *Cutz*, *Bangz*, *Trendz*, *Sparx* and *Beautyworx*. These examples are all from the USA, but similar examples could be found anywhere in the English-speaking world. British fish-and-chip shops also seem to have a penchant for spelling-based puns, as we see in these London venues: *Ace Plaice*, *Happy Plaice*, *My Plaice*, *Fry-Days*, *Friars Inn* and *Supa Fry*. (Completely off-topic, but irresistible: in trawling through the London directory of fish-and-chip shops I came across the wonderfully named *Oh My Cod*.)

But there is a second reason for non-standard spelling in trade names: the need to distinguish a name from some other similarly named product. If a firm already exists called *Quality Curtains*, then you or I can become a competitor by calling ourselves *Kwality Kurtains*. Or, if we are unsure whether a name already exists, we can minimise the risk of a clash by opting for a deviant spelling at the outset. That is why we find so many racehorses with distinctive names, such as *Adorabull*, *Hugs and Kysses*, *Citi Centre*, *Tyme After Tyme* and – perhaps most famous of all – *Phar Lap*. Animals seem to be a particular source of spelling deviance. Among the long lists of cat names we find *Allie Cat*, *Aristakat* and *Baggi Pants*. Among the names people have given their pet parrots are

Chirpee, Koconut and *Wisper*. Sometimes an organisation tries to control naming, thus motivating the creation of even more outlandish spellings. Newly accepted names in 2011 by the Kennel Club in Britain included *Atkat, Stormefex, Naefela* and *Deuceshi*.

We are talking about identity now. The more an individual or group wants to appear different from the rest of society, the more likely we are to encounter a non-standard spelling. Pop groups and rap artists are among the leaders, in this respect. A random selection from contemporary listings includes (for groups) *Sugababes, Boyzone, Gorillaz* and *Deftones*, and (for rappers) *Ginuwine, Ice Dogg, Kaos* and *Dizzee Rascal*. Tribute bands have a special problem, as a consequence. They need to find a distinctive spelling that reminds their fans of the original name (which is itself often spelled in a non-standard way) and yet differs from it. Thus we find the original *Beatles* (a combination of *beetles* and *beat*) echoed in bands which have called themselves *Beatals, Beatalls, Beatels* and then – with the wheel turning full circle – *Beetles*.

Anyone can play with spelling in this way. House-names provide a rich source of examples: *Adenuf, All-wynds, Ardgraft, At-Om-Ere* … K rears its head again with such formations as *Kozy Kot, Kozikorner* and *Kozinuk*. Archaisms appear: *Olde Forge, Faerie Cottage*. Archaic spellings, of course, can turn up in any social setting, such as *summer fayres, olde tyme dances* and various kinds of *shoppe*. Shoppes are no longer limited to places where the traditional is being emphasised (*Ye Olde Pork Pie Shoppe, Heritage Shoppe*) but, especially in the USA, are found in all sorts of modern settings (*Comix Shoppe, Lollipop Shoppe* and the linguistically mind-boggling *Rifle Shoppe*).

To the learner, all this spelling variation must be somewhat confusing. If one has become a good speller, then one can easily see the joke when fish-and-chip shops go by such names as *Friar Tuck, Fryer Tuck* or *Frier Tuck*. But if one is trying to make sense of an already complex spelling system, this kind of punful diversity must be a hindrance rather than a help. What is the standard spelling of 'something that fries'? After seeing such variation, even a mature speller can be knocked off-balance.

What is especially surprising is to see this kind of deviance in books for beginner readers. Children's authors seem to go out of their way to find weird spellings for their characters' names, and to spell their words in weird ways. While I am all for variety and innovation in early reading materials, there must surely be a problem when children who have not yet mastered the basic patterns of the spelling system are introduced to rare or impossible letter sequences. There are hardly any words in English beginning with *wu, kw* or *skr*, for example, but Dr Seuss gives us such names as *Wumbus* and *Wump*, *Kweet* and *Kwigger*, *Skring* and *Skritz*. *Skritz* is doubly unfamiliar, as hardly any words in English end with *tz*. The only word in English begining with *zl* is the loanword *zloty*, but Dr Seuss creates *Zlock*. There are no words at all ending in *rll* or *wf*, but he gives us *Thwerll* and *Dawf*. A double-*k* sequence is uncommon (thanks to the replacement by *ck*; see Chapter 7), but we find *Glikker* and *Yekko*. A final *x* or *v* is rare (Chapter 8), but we see *Lorax, Zax, Gox, Grox* and the *Snuvs. Snuvs*, moreover, is made to rhyme with *gloves*.

Clearly the author wants names which sound or look strange, and mature readers respond well to them. I delight in every one of the names I've just listed. But there is surely a problem for young children who love to hear these stories read aloud, and who want to read them themselves, while at the same time struggling to make sense of the English spelling system. It is an unnecessary barrier. How are they supposed to work out which is the basic pattern when *Snuvs* and *gloves* are before their eyes as equals? It is perfectly possible to have weird names which respect the basic patterns of English spelling, such as Dr Seuss's *Grinch, Gootch, Flustard, Chuggs* and *Preep*. And it is good pedagogy to introduce non-standard spellings in contrast with the standard norm, as the contrast helps to establish the difference between standard and non-standard in the child's mind. This is what A. A. Milne does in his Winnie-the-Pooh stories: *hunny* appears only after *honey* is introduced, *wol* after *owl, piglit* after *piglet*. That is a good way to reinforce the notion that non-standard spellings are the exception rather than the rule, and are there for special effect.

It is an important lesson to learn, as the contrast

between standard and non-standard spelling is a major feature of creative writing. Writers want to give local colour to what their characters say, so they adopt non-standard spellings to reflect the way they speak. The spellings can reflect a regional origin, as with *yer* for *your*, *reet* for *right*, or *thowt* for *thought*. They can be simply a reflection of a rapid colloquial speech style, as with *gotcha* ('got you'), *gimme* ('give me'), *wanna* ('want to'), *kinda* ('kind of') and *outta* ('out of'). They can point to a class distinction: people from many social backgrounds pronounce *was* as /wɒz/, but if it is written *woz* there is a definite lower-class implication – and the same applies to several other spellings, such as *wot* for *what*, *bin* for *been*, and *Missus* for *Mrs*. We see hundreds of non-standard forms in the novels of Charles Dickens, Emily Brontë, Walter Scott and Mark Twain, and in the writing of the 19th-century American humorists Artemus Ward (aka Charles Farrar Browne) and Josh Billings (aka Henry Wheeler Shaw), we find non-standard spelling throughout their entire oeuvre. 'It is tru,' says Josh Billings, 'that welth won't maik a man vartuous, but i notis thare ain't enyboddy who wants tew be poor jist for the purpiss ov being good.' Nor do children have to wait until they grow up to encounter characters using non-standard spelling, as a glance at the pages of Richmal Crompton (e.g. William) or J. K. Rowling (e.g. Hagrid) shows.

31
Unpredictability

Identity is especially relevant in the names of people and places, which are often written in an idiosyncratic way. They provide English with some of its most irregular and unpredictable spellings.

We need an orthography to be predictable. There has to be a systematic relationship between sounds and letters. In a perfectly phonetic spelling system, the relationship is one-to-one: each sound is represented by one letter, so that it can be easily written, and each letter is pronounced with one sound, so that it can be easily read. Some languages, such as Welsh and Spanish, come very close to this goal, and some words in English are indeed highly predictable: nobody has a problem reading or writing such words as *hat, men, pram* or *strips*. However, as we have seen, most English words are only partially predictable.

The problem is easier for the reader than for the writer. As already mentioned in Chapter 6, if we are presented with, say, *beet*, there is really only one way to say it: /biːt/. But presented with the sound sequence /biːt/ and asked to write it down, it could be

any one of several spellings – *beat, beet, bete, biet, beete*
… The way English spelling has developed makes
some of these spellings more likely than others, but
the vagaries of the system mean that none is ruled
out. Also, changes in vocabulary over time mean that
it is always possible for a new word to arrive which
uses a previously non-existent spelling. There is no
word *biet* in English – yet. And, as nobody knows
all the words in English, it is always possible that a
word considered non-existent actually does exist in
a regional dialect or a specialist field. Most people
would reject *bete* as a word – but it's listed in the
Oxford English Dictionary as a variant spelling of *beet*,
used in some dialects (such as Scotland) with the
meaning of 'mend' or 'repair'. And there are several
people in the telephone directory with the surname
Beete.

Proper names are where things get really tough
for the English speller, for it is here that we find
instances of the worst-case scenario: virtually total
unpredictability. When we hear a name, there is no
guarantee that its spelling will be anything like how
it is spoken. In Norfolk you will hear people talking
about going to /eɪzbrə/. Only familiarity with the
locale would enable you to relate this to what you
see on a signpost: *Happisburgh*. On another signpost
you will see *Wymondham*, but you have to know that
it is pronounced /wɪndəm/. Some of the really idiosyncratic spellings are so well known that we tend to
forget just how irregular they are – *Gloucester* /glɒstə/,

Leicester /l<u>es</u>tə/ or *Leominster* /<u>lem</u>stə/, for example –
but they all have to be learned, by natives and foreign
visitors alike. And there are many unique forms. No
other English word looks like *Seend*, in Wiltshire.

Personal names can be even more of a problem.
Surnames are especially unpredictable, given the ancient spelling traditions that run in some families.
Famous cases include *Featherstonehaugh*, pronounced
like 'fanshaw' /f<u>æn</u>ʃɔ:/, and *Cholmondeley*, pronounced
like 'chumley' /ʧʌmlɪ/, but there are many oth-
ers, such as *Knollys*, pronounced like 'Knowles'
/nəʊlz/, and *Sandys*, pronounced like 'Sands'
/sændz/. Novelist P. G. Wodehouse, pronounced like
'woodhouse' /wʊdhaʊs/, had some fun with this feature of British eccentricity in his books about Ru-
pert Psmith. In Chapter 31 of *Psmith, Journalist*, the
eponymous hero is asked for his name.

> 'I am Psmith,' said the old Etonian reverently.
> 'There is a preliminary P before the name. This,
> however, is silent. Like the tomb. Compare such
> words as ptarmigan, psalm, and phthisis.'

It could have been worse. His first name might have
been *Ralph*, pronounced 'Rafe' /reɪf/.

We cannot ignore such items, in an account of
English spelling. Just because they are names does
not let us off the hook. We still have to read them
and write them. There is no alternative but to learn
them by heart, and to be prepared for the unexpected.
People who have names with an unpredictable spelling know this, and become used to spelling out their

name when occasion demands it. 'It's Elisabeth with an s', 'That's Browne with an e'. I am one: 'That's Crystal, C R Y S T A L'. I did once try saying, 'Crystal, as in Swarovski', but nobody got the point.

Browne illustrates a general point. Many surnames have developed a distinctive spelling in order to differentiate the name from a common word in the language. Adding a final *e* is a regular strategy, as we see in Messrs *Frye*, *Cooke* and *Younge*. Doubling the final consonant is another strategy, as Messrs *Carr*, *Hogg* and *Webb* illustrate. Changing *i* to *y* is also popular, as with Messrs *Taylor*, *Cryer* and *Pye*. And of course we find names which use two of these strategies in combination, as with Messrs *Legge*, *Crabbe* and *Donne* or *Smythe*, *Wylde* and *Blythe*. A surname may even use all three, as with *Thynne*.

Unusual double-letter sequences may also show the influence of other languages, such as the initial *ll* seen in *Lloyd* and *Llewelyn* (from Welsh). Initial *ff* is also sometimes seen in Welsh-derived names (*Ffion*, *Ffrancon*), because double *f* is a letter in the Welsh alphabet (representing /f/), contrasting with a single *f* (representing /v/), and some Welsh people have extended the practice to other names (*Ffred*, *Ffrancis*). A double *f* is also seen in some English names (*Ffoulkes*, *Fforde*, *Ffrench*, *Ffitch*), deriving from an early scribal practice of writing a capital *F* as *ff*. The awkward appearance of *Ff*, along with an upper-class penchant for idiosyncrasy, led to the highly unusual practice of using the lower-case letters for the surname, resulting in such forms as *ffoulkes* and *ffrench*, still occasionally seen today.

These examples suggest that the spelling rules that apply to words in the dictionary don't apply to the proper names of the encyclopaedic world. In these names we see forms which are rare in general orthography (such as the *ae* of *Michael* or *Rachael*) or which never became general practice (such as the bicapitalisation of *FitzMaurice* and *McMillan*, or the interpolated punctuation of *O'Malley* and *D'Eath*). But this kind of unpredictability can sometimes be encountered in dictionary words too, when we borrow not just a foreign word but its spelling as well.

Ogden Nash on names

Not only can I not remember anecdotes that are racy
But I also can't remember whether the names of my Scottish friends
    begin with M-c or M-a-c,
And I can't speak for you, but for myself there is one dilemma with me
    in the middle of it,
Which is, is it Katharine with a K or Catherine with a C, and furthermore
    is it an A or is it an E in the middle of it?
I can remember the races between Man o' War and Sir Barton, and
    Epinard and Zev,
But I can't remember whether it's Johnson or Johnston any more than
    whether you address a minister as Mr. or Dr. or simply Rev.
I know a cygnet from a gosling and a coney from a leveret,
But how to distinguish an I-double-T from an E-double-T Everett?
I am familiar with the nature of an oath,
But I get confused between the Eliot with one L and one T, and the
    Elliot with two L's and one T, and the Eliott with one L and two T's,
    and the Elliott with two of both.
How many of my friendships have lapsed because of an extra T or a
    missing L;
Give me a simple name like Taliaferro or Wambsganss or Torporcer or
    Joralemon or Mankiewicz that any schoolboy can spell,
Because many former friends thought I was being impolite to them
When it was only because I couldn't remember whether they were
    Stuarts with a U or Stewarts with an E-W that I didn't write to them.

('What's in a name? Some letter I always forget',
in *The Private Dining Room*, 1952)

32

Exotic vowels

A dramatic shift in the character of English spelling has come about through loanwords where an effort has been made to preserve their exotic character. The effect can often be seen in the vowels.

From the viewpoint of spelling, loanwords are of several kinds. In many cases, a foreign word arrives and is spelled according to the normal conventions of English. When Irish *seamrog* arrived in English towards the end of the 16th century, after a period of variation it settled down as *shamrock*. Nothing unusual there. Nor is there anything especially unusual about the spelling of *wigwam, bandit, monsoon* and many more loans which arrived at that time. This is what we would expect. As long as there was no risk of uncertainty about meaning or pronunciation, there was no reason for English writers to follow the foreign spellings, with their unfamiliar letters, letter combinations and diacritics.

Things didn't stay that way, though. When German *Nudel* arrived in the late 18th century it was immediately spelled *noodle*, following other words in which a long /uː/ vowel sound was spelled *oo* and /əl/ endings spelled *le*. However, a century later, German *Strudel* didn't receive the same treatment: British menus offer *apple strudel*, never *apple stroodle*. And today we find our lexicon littered with exotic spellings, such as *ciao* for a farewell (when we would expect something like *chow*), *film noir* (when we would expect something like *nwahr*), and *taoiseach* for the Irish prime minister (when we would expect something like *teeshuck*). In the last century or so, the preference to keep the spelling of the source language has become a major feature of the writing system, and some very strange-looking spellings are the result. Modern loanwords now account for much of the unpredictability of English spelling.

We have got used to the oldest arrivals, of course. Nobody really thinks of such words as *army* and *navy*, *judge* and *jury* or *roast* and *beef*, all borrowed from French in the Middle Ages, as loanwords. They've been with us too long, and their spelling has assimilated to English norms. It's the later loans from languages further afield, especially those encountered during the period of the growing British Empire, that present the biggest problem. Here we find all kinds of new spellings, with both vowels and consonants affected.

We are used to the notion that there are five written vowels in English: A, E, I, O, U. But if loanwords are taken into account, we have at least seven, for W and Y appear in several cases. In Britain, people especially notice loans from Welsh because Wales is geographically so close, which include such words as *Llyn*, 'lake' or *Cwm*, 'valley'. Both vowel letters are seen in *hwyl* 'emotional fervour'. The total could be larger than seven if we count vowels with accents as different. Is the *é* in *café* a different letter from the *e* in *chef*, and different again from the *è* of *learnèd* and the *ê* of *bête noire*? Even *r* can act as a vowel, if you're wanting to represent such sounds as *Brrr* (Chapter 34), or travelling to the Croatian island of *Krk*.

There is quite a bit of variant usage: we will see such words as *matinee, soiree, melee* and *puree* both with and without accents. Some of the French words also give us an additional spelling complication, presenting us with the option of reflecting French grammatical gender. The only word which regularly makes the distinction is *fiancé* vs. *fiancée*, but some writers insist on maintaining it with *blond* vs. *blonde*, and it is sometimes seen in such words as *confidant(e)*, *protégé(e)*, *attaché(e)* and *chargé(e) d'affaires*.

We also find the basic five vowel letters used in unusual combinations and in unusual positions. Unusual combinations? Doubling is normal with *e* and *o*, as we saw in Chapter 5, but not with the other three: words like *aardvark, bazaar, leylandii* and *muumuu* strike us as alien. We also find something which is rare in English: a sequence of *three* vowel letters, as in *taoiseach* and *rooibos*. Or four in the case of *Hawaiian*.

As for unusual positions, one of the most

noticeable features of loanwords since the Renaissance is the large number which end in a single sounded vowel letter. Double vowel letters at the end of a word are familiar enough with *ee* and *oo* (*tree, too*), and a silent final *e* is an important signal of vowel length, as we saw in Chapter 6. But a single sounded vowel letter at the end of a word looks a little odd: *saga, cantata, taffeta; forte, dilettante, hyperbole; alkali, ravioli, sari; volcano, potato, concerto; menu, babu, coypu.* Some of these (*potato, tomato, piano,* etc.) are now so familiar that we would hardly think of them as exotic today; but we unconsciously recall their alien character when we try to form their plurals. We form a normal plural in English by 'adding an *s*'. But when people first wrote *menus, pianos, tomatos* and suchlike, they felt uncomfortable with the result. The words didn't look right. *Menus* looks like a combination of *men + us,* to be pronounced 'menuss'. *Tomatos* looked like *toma + toss.*

Spellings like *tomatos* were in fact used in earlier centuries, but over time the discomfort led to alternatives. Some nouns ending in *-o* followed the practice of nouns ending in *-y* (*story > stories*) by adding an *-es,* so we see *potatoes, tomatoes, volcanoes, echoes* and a few more. But the practice was never introduced systematically, so we also find *solos, folios, oratorios* and others. As a result, there is a huge amount of variation, with dictionaries and online guides sometimes accepting both alternatives (e.g. *mosquitos* and *mosquitoes*), and sometimes making conflicting recommendations (one source advises *stilettoes,* another *stilettos*). When Standard English can't make its mind up, it's hardly surprising to find people opting for non-standard solutions – in this case, the so-called 'greengrocer's apostrophe', as in *potato's* and *tomato's,* which signals that the following *s* is a plural ending and not part of the basic word. It's an understandable error, though one which is widely condemned. The penalty for not using the apostrophe, however, is an extra load on the memory. We now have to remember which -*o* words add an -*es* and which don't.

With only five (or so) vowel letters to worry about, exotic spelling adaptations are fairly limited. With over twenty consonant letters available, the range of spelling variations is very much greater.

Disenvowelling

The town we landed at was named Guayaquerita, so they told me. 'Not for me,' says I. 'It'll be little old Hilldale or Tompkinsville or Cherry Tree Corners when I speak of it. It's a clear case where Spelling Reform ought to butt in and disenvowel it.'

(O Henry, 'A ruler of men', from *Rolling Stones*, 1906)

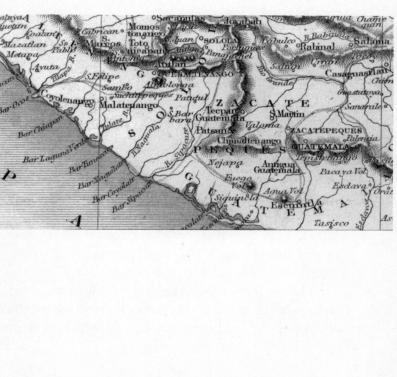

33
Exotic consonants

The character of English spelling has been especially affected by the way loanwords have adapted the consonant system. They reinforce the point that the choice of a spelling is not simply a linguistic issue, but a matter of identity.

What new spellings affect consonants? As with vowels, loanwords have altered their number, combination and position. New consonant letters appear whenever a loan keeps the diacritic used with the letter from the source alphabet. A *c* with a cedilla can be seen in some loans from French, such as *façade*. Other examples include *ł*, *č* and *ñ*. Today, we tend not to use diacritics unless there is a special need to show a difference in meaning – as in the case of *resume* vs. *résumé* – or to remind us of a pronunciation, as with *matinée*, or the name of Karel *Čapek* (pronounced 'cha-pek'), who introduced us to the word *robot* in the 1920s.

The original pronunciation is usually disregarded when we see an unfamiliar diacritic: when we see the Polish city of *Lodz* written as *Łodz*, English speakers

typically ignore the distinctive phonetic value represented by the Ł, and say it in an English way, as 'Lods'.
(It's actually pronounced more like 'Woodge'.) The
same thing happens when they see letter pairs which
represent single consonant sounds in the source
language. Welsh again provides British people with
examples, as they encounter *dd* representing /ð/ in
such words as *eisteddfod* and *ll* representing a voiceless *l* in *Llandudno* and many other place names. The
usual English pronunciation replaces the *dd* with a
/d/ and the *ll* with an /l/ or /kl/. Welsh people can
get very cross about it.

Particularly important is the way loanwords
manipulate English consonants, pushing them into
unfamiliar positions and combining them in unfamiliar ways. Unfamiliar positions? We are used to
seeing -*ng* at the ends of words (*bang, sing, running*)
but not at the beginning, as in the currency unit of
Bhutan, the *ngultrum*, or the New Zealand evergreen,
the *ngaio*. A double l is likewise familiar at the end of
a word (*full, tell, ill*) but not at the beginning (*llama,
llano*). Similarly, we don't expect to see a *j* at the end
of a word, but we will find them in some words relating to institutions in India, such as *samaj, swaraj* and
raj. And, as already noted in Chapter 8, a final *v* was
avoided by the French scribes, so that modern loans
such as *Slav, Kalashnikov* and *Chicken Kiev* look alien.
So do words ending in a single *k*, as in *anorak, appa-
ratchik* and *trek*, or *z*, as in *fez, Tammuz* and *pince-nez*.

Unfamiliar combinations? We see these especially

244 Spell it out

at the beginning of words: a random sample would be *Knesset, ptarmigan, sgraffito, svelte, sjambok, kvetch, czar / tzar, zloty* and *tsunami*. Several loans show a consonant followed by *h*, either at the beginning of a word, as in *bhaji, dhow, khaki, rhinoceros* and *zho*, or at the end, as in *ceilidh, ankh* and *sheikh*. Unusual doublings are seen in a few loans relating to Islam, such as *hajj, qawwali* and *Umayyad*. *Schmaltz, chintz* and *veldt* are examples of unusual final three-consonant combinations. Russian or German loans such as *bortsch, putsch* and *shchi* (a type of cabbage soup from Russia) show a distinctive four-consonant sequence.

With some loans, vowels and consonants combine to give an unusual appearance to the whole word, and an unpredictable pronunciation, as in the case of *pharaoh, daguerreotype, boutique* and *dahlia*. In one case, the failure of a consonant to combine with a vowel is the distinctive feature: *q* without its accompanying *u*, as in *qi* and *qigong* from Chinese and *qadi* and *qasida* from Arabic.

Exotic words also account for many of the words which have alternative spellings. Look at the menu in different Indian restaurants and you will see *popadoms, poppadums, popadums, papadoms, poppodoms, poppadams* and other variants. People practise *t'ai chi, tai chi* or *taiqi*. They eat *lichis, lychees, lichees* or *litchis*; *yoghurt, yogurt, yogourt* or *yoghourt*; *hummus, houmous, hummos, hummous* or *humus*. Food words are especially prone to variation, as there is a strong disposition to make menus look suitably ethnic, and people make different decisions about how this is to be achieved.

Sometimes parts of the English-using world go in different directions. *Yogurt* is the norm in the USA. In the UK, *yoghurt* is three times more common than *yogurt*. *Yogourt* has achieved some presence in Canada, because of its French-looking character, but even there *yogurt* is more widespread. In Australia and New Zealand, *yoghurt* is more frequent than *yogurt*, but *yogurt* is catching up, probably because of exposure to American and Internet usage. *Yogurt* is catching up in the UK too.

When exotic words retain an idiosyncratic spelling, we are sometimes at a loss to know how to pronounce them. The strategies we have painfully learned over the years no longer apply. When we encounter such forms as *jojoba, feng shui* and *uillean pipes* for the first time, we can do no more than make a brave guess. And, as a result, some loanwords have developed variant pronunciations, such as *dachshund, chutzpah, loch, finale, houdah, agouti* and *gnocchi*. Familiarity breeds content, in such cases – we no longer have any problem over such unique forms as *canoe* or *lasso* – but it may take a while for other loans to achieve this comfortable state.

The variant spellings in loanwords reinforce an important fact: the choice of a spelling is not simply a linguistic matter, but a question of identity. Just as Noah Webster wanted to reform British spelling to symbolise his new nation (Chapter 26) and various groups have adopted a particular spelling to reflect a specific tradition (Chapter 28), so the spelling of a loanword can represent an important political, ethnic, religious or professional distinction. For example, most people write *taboo*, but if we see *tabu*, then we are probably reading something by an anthropologist. In British English, most people write *programme*, unless they are in the world of computing, in which case it is *program*. The point extends to all words, not just loanwords. Most people vary between *judgement* and *judgment*, but judges making a decision always use *judgment*. The difference between a specialised and a non-specialised or colloquial style is also sometimes visible in the spelling, as in the contrast between *vocal cords* (the only spelling recognised in phonetics) and *vocal chords*, or *lunatic* and *loony* (not *luny*).

The issues are especially noticeable with the names of people or groups. Welsh people may decide to use *Harri* and *Huw* for *Harry* and *Hugh*. Irish people may opt for *Caireann* rather than *Karen* or *Ó Dónaill* rather than *O'Donnell*. An East European immigrant family may name their child *Aleksander* rather than *Alexander*. Countries may choose a new spelling upon achieving independence (as with *Guyana*, formerly *British Guiana*), or a group may prefer one spelling rather than another (as when the Australian *Labour* Party changed its spelling to *Labor*). The choices may prove controversial, and raise issues of political correctness, as with *Beijing* vs. *Peking*, *Hawaii* vs. *Hawai'i* or *gipsy* vs. *gypsy*.

In some cases, the desire to respect local identities has resulted in a spelling simplification. The spelling of the sound /f/ by *ph* is largely associated with loanwords from Greek, as with *philosophy, phallic, phenotype* and *telephone*. But when Greek cheese arrived in British restaurants in the 20th century, it was spelled *feta* not *pheta*, and similarly we see such forms as *fava, fasolakia, fakkes* and *pilafi*. However, celebration for this apparent gain among spelling reformers would be premature, for we see a counter-trend in recent years with *ph* replacing *f* to express such new concepts as *phoods* (foods offering pharmaceutical benefits) and *phishing* (online masquerading). Charles Storch, in the *Chicago Tribune* (20 April 2004), was one who noticed the new fashion. In an article headed 'Not so phast', he wrote:

> Perfectly good English words are getting a meaning makeover when their beginning letter 'f' is substituted with 'ph.' Think of 'phat,' 'phishing' and 'phood' and you might wonder what the 'ph' is going on.

An apposite comment for English spelling as a whole, some might think.

The spread of education

THE SPREAD OF EDUCATION

"Come and 'ave a look, Marier. They've been and put a chick on a lidy's 'at, and they don't know 'ow to spell it!"

(From *Mr Punch with the Children, c.* 1900, p. 126)

34

Spelling noises

We also need to spell the emotional noises that form a part of conversation. A phonetic spelling turns out not to be so easy to achieve.

Spoken language is more than words and sentences. It also contains quite a few isolated noises which are used to express emotions. Grammarians call them *interjections*. If we want to write them down – as we would in a novel, a comic-book or an email – we have to find a way of spelling them and it's not always obvious how to do so. A phonetic spelling is not always possible.

The chief problem is that many of these noises use sounds that aren't part of the normal set of English vowels and consonants. Take the sound we use when we want to draw someone's attention to the fact that we're there, or we disapprove of what they've just said. It's actually a clearing of the throat. How is this to be spelled? The earliest versions, in the 18th century, record it as *Hem!*, and today it's usually spelled *Ahem!* It's not a bad representation, but we still need to learn the conventional spelling.

If we want a character to convey throat-clearing, it would be no good writing *Eham*, *Mhumh* or some other – only *Ahem* will do.

Quite a few interjections are like this. We use sounds at the back of our mouth to express various kinds of disgust, and these are only roughly indicated by such spellings as *yuk*, *argh*, *ugh* and *blech*. We produce sounds using both lips to express a range of emotions such as relief, astonishment and dismay, and write these down approximately as *phew*, *whew* or *pff*. And we produce a click noise with our tongue against the upper teeth ridge to express disapproval or irritation. This is usually written as *tut* – a spelling known since the 16th century – but other spellings have appeared as people try to get the effect down on paper. Rudyard Kipling, for example, spelled it as *tck*. In the 1940s, *tsk* became popular. That may be phonetically more accurate, but orthographically it breaks all the rules. For now we have 'words' without any vowel letters at all.

Tsk is not alone. Think of *brr* ('I'm cold'), *grr* ('I'm cross'), *sh* ('be quiet'), *pst* ('I'm trying to get your attention surreptitiously') and *hm* ('I'm thinking'), as well as the conversational noises of agreement such as *m* and *mhm*. No vowel letters anywhere. And the number of consonant letters can increase, depending on the intensity of the sound to be conveyed. How cross are you? *Grrrr!* How cold? *Brrrrr!* How quiet? *Psssst!* How meditative? *Hmmmm.* The length of a vowel sound can even be shown by increasing the number of consonant letters. *Aw* expresses a wide range of mild emotions, such as entreaty, sympathy and disapproval. It's just a long vowel sound, but if you make it longer, the way to spell it is not *aaaw*, but *awww*. *Ow* is similar: *Owww!* On the other hand, we increase the intensity of *ah* by writing *aaah* not *ahhh*, and *eek* by *eeek* not *eekkk*.

Spelling variants also exist. The conversation agreement noise is sometimes written *m*, sometimes *mm*. *Yuk* appears as *yuck*. We find *hmph* and *humph*, *oops* and *whoops*. *Ow* has a *w*, but the identical sound in *ouch* has a *u*. There's also language change. *Pshaw* has been in written English since the 17th century, but seems to be on its way out today. And new interjections have appeared, such as *mwah* (for air-kissing), *phwoar* (enthusiastic affirmation, especially of sexual attractiveness), and the interjection made famous by Homer Simpson (though long predating him) to express an awareness that one has done something stupid: *d'oh*. Here too there are variants: *doh*, *dooh*, *duh* and *duhh*.

Then there are the interjections which seem to have no phonetic basis whatsoever. We do not actually go *boo-hoo* when crying, nor *bah* when disgusted, nor *yikes* when we get into trouble (as comic-book characters do). But here the wheel turns full circle. Simply because these are the conventional ways of writing these noises down, when reading them aloud people tend to follow the spelling, and pronounce the words as they look. So we will hear

/bu: hu:/, with the vowels and consonants articulated clearly – totally unlike what happens when we cry. The same thing has happened to several other interjections. If we like what we're eating (or, sometimes, seeing), we can say *yum yum*. If we get excited, especially when moving downwards at speed, we can say *wheeee*. People happily articulate *yuk* without us hearing any saliva rushing about the back of the throat. We hear *brr* sounding like *burr*, without the lips trembling, and – the best example to my mind of pronunciation trying to follow the spelling – we hear people adding a vowel and saying *tusk tusk*.

Unspellable noises

CECILY: [taking dictation] Oh, don't cough, Ernest. When one is dictating one should speak fluently and not cough. Besides, I don't know how to spell a cough.

(Oscar Wilde, *The Importance of Being Earnest*, 1895, Act 2)

35

Abbreviating

*Spelling involves more than learning to read and write
whole words; we also need to handle the abbreviations
and symbols which play an important role in several
everyday orthographic situations. A surprising amount of
inconsistency is encountered.*

The primary aim of a standard spelling system is
to promote mutual intelligibility. If we all learn the
same system, then we can read what anyone writes
(in the broadest sense, to include typing and printing). But writing and reading involve more than
intelligibility. We want to be able to write efficiently,
avoiding unnecessary labour. We want to be able to
read comfortably and with pleasure. And our written
output needs to look good – or, at least, to avoid a
graphic appearance that hinders our achievement of
these goals. Spelling practice may be affected by all
these considerations.

Abbreviation is the most important factor. Spelling involves not only knowing how to deal with
words when they are written in full but also when
they are shortened. We need to learn that *Doctor* can

be reduced to *Dr* and not *D* or *Dcr* or some other form, and that we must shorten *mile* to *mi*, not *ml* (which is *millilitre*). We need to know that it is routine practice to write *am* and *pm* and never *ante meridiem* ('before midday') and *post meridiem* ('after midday'). We need to know that we can 'spell' *hundredweight* as the unpronounceable *cwt*, and be aware of the relationship between *pound* and *lb*, *ounce* and *oz*, *kilometre* and *km*, *quarter* and *qtr*, and many more. The problem is sometimes greater for the reader than the writer. It is not difficult to take a name, such as *Irish Republican Army*, and abbreviate it to *IRA*; the learning task is to know whether this should be read letter-by-letter (like *BBC*) or as a complete word (like *NATO*) or as a hybrid (like *CD-ROM*).

'Logograms' also play a part in the English writing system: these are cases where a word is not just shortened, but entirely replaced by a symbol. Examples include @ for 'at', £ for 'pound', % for 'per cent' and + for 'plus'. The ampersand, &, is one of the oldest. It is a collapsed version of the Latin word *et*, 'and': the bottom circle is what's left of the *e*, and the rising tail on the right is what's left of the *t*. Numerals are another kind of logogram: we read *1*, *2*, *3*, etc. as 'one, two, three …' And it is part of the business of learning to read and write to know when we should write words in their logographic form and when to spell them out.

This turns out to be trickier than at first appears, especially with numerals. Some situations are clear:

nobody would ever write out a telephone number or a postal address in full form. We never see the following:

John Doe
One hundred and thirty-two Doe Street
Brooklyn
New York one one two four three

That is the sort of thing we say, but we always write:

John Doe
132 Doe Street
Brooklyn
New York 11243

The point seems obvious, but it still has to be learned. Such conventions are usually taught in school, though teachers rarely draw attention to the spelling implications.

Other contexts where numerals are normal are the expression of percentages and decimals, currency amounts, recipe quantities and dates:

Around 3 per cent of the population ...
It cost me £5.
Add 2 spoonfuls of salt ...
On 31 January 2012 ...

However, other contexts are not so straightforward. Which of the following should we write?

I can see three stars.
I can see 3 stars.

I can see thirty-three stars.
I can see 33 stars.

I can see three thousand stars.
I can see 3 thousand stars.
I can see 3,000 stars.

I can see three million stars.
I can see 3 million stars.
I can see 3,000,000 stars.

Style guides and publishers' house styles vary in their recommendations. Some say that a numeral should always be spelled out up to ten; others up to a hundred. Some say that if a numeral is spoken as a single word, then it should be spelled out – so, *thirteen, fourteen, twenty, thirty* and *ninety*, but *21, 43, 96* ... Others disagree, and advise *13, 14, 20, 30* and *90*. Some insist that numerals above a million are spelled out, so we should write *3 million* not *three million*, but *3,000* not *3 thousand*. All say that, whatever the choices we make, we should be consistent. Usage also varies with currencies. If we read 'It cost $3.50 / £3.50' we have several options in saying this aloud:

It cost three fifty.
It cost three dollars fifty / three pound(s) fifty.
It cost three dollars fifty cents / three pounds fifty
   pence.
It cost three dollars and fifty cents / three pounds
   and fifty pence.

Note that the dollar and pound signs come first in writing, but are said second in speech. We cannot say:

> It cost dollars three fifty / It cost pounds three fifty.

Here too the problem is more for the reader than the writer. After writing $3.50 or £3.50, the job is done. For the reader, the job is just beginning. Similarly, readers have to know that, when seeing a date such as *31 January*, a possible spoken correlative is 'the 31st of January'; when reading *Richard III*, they can say 'Richard the third'. And when writing, it is important to know that they must not write *Richard the third*, *Richard the 3rd*, and other possibilities. They have to know when to insert the 'ghost' words, such as *the* and *of*.

On top of all this there are the rules introduced by printers on functional grounds. One such rule says we must avoid juxtaposing numerals in their logographic form: we should not write such expressions as *The class contains 15 16-year-old children*. One or other of the words should be spelled out – or the sentence rephrased, of course. Another rule is that a sentence should not begin with a numeral. Since the 19th century, generations of children have been taught never to write like this:

> 30 per cent of the population live by the river.

Rather it should be:

> Thirty per cent of the population live by the river.

The practice originated because printers felt that, if numerals were allowed in an initial position, it would be difficult to see where one sentence ended and the next began. With letters there is no such problem, because we start a sentence with a capital letter – but there are no 'capital numerals'. The rule nonetheless has often been broken, and these days we often see numeral-initial sentences, especially on the Internet.

Despite the best efforts of printers, publishers and stylists, there is still a great deal of variation. Do we write, referring to years, *the 80s* or *the eighties*? Do we write that someone won *1st prize* or *first prize*? And what do we do when a word reaches the end of a line and, in justified setting, has to be broken to make it fit. Where does the hyphen go? There are major differences in spelling practice between British and American English. On the whole, British English printers insert the hyphen to separate the meaningful elements of a word, following etymology (*know-ledge, inform-ation*); American printers follow the word's sound structure, inserting the hyphen between syllables (*knowl-edge, infor-mation*). Dictionaries and publishers' house styles provide guidance, but practice varies a great deal, on both sides of the Atlantic.

Abbreviations are a major component of the English writing system, not a marginal feature. The largest dictionaries of abbreviations contain well over half a million entries, and their number is increasing all the time. The various forms of electronic communication have given a new lease of life to several old forms, such as *c* for *see* and *2* for *to*, and they are an important characteristic of text-messaging and tweeting, where the number of characters in a message is limited.

A popular myth of the early 2000s was that these substitutions were promoting illiteracy among young people. The reality is that this kind of language play actually enhances it. You have to have learned a great deal about the spelling system of English in order to text well. Considerable linguistic awareness lies behind the apparently simple task of spelling *see you later* as *c u l8er*. Texters have to make a judgement about which letters can be safely eliminated without harming the recognisability of the words. Nobody texts by leaving out all the consonants. If we take a sentence such as *don't forget to bring your passport*, we are likely to see a version like this on the Internet:

dnt frgt 2 brng yr passprt

but never a version like this:

o oe 2 i ou ao

It's actually quite tricky to write a heavily abbreviated sentence so that people will be able to read and understand it. And, of course, if it is 'cool' to leave letters out, texters have to know that the letters are there in the first place in order to leave them out. Unsurprisingly, then, the best texters and tweeters turn out to be the best spellers.

36

Learning the system

*Basic linguistic principles can help to show a system
behind the apparent arbitrariness of English spelling.
Three such principles are illustrated and applied to some
famous 'difficult' spellings.*

So how does one become a 'best speller'? It is clear
that traditional proposals haven't worked. The 'solution' suggested by the etymologists of the 16th
century (Chapter 21) succeeded only in increasing
the amount of irregularity in the language. The 'rules'
introduced by teachers in the 19th century proved
too simplified to handle the many apparent exceptions (Chapter 24). The radical arguments presented
by spelling reformers have never persuaded, with the
sole exception of Noah Webster (Chapter 26). As a
result, learning to spell English today seems just as
hard as it ever was. There is still a huge amount to
learn. But with a modicum of awareness about the
nature of language in general and of the spelling
system in particular, the task can be eased.

The operative word is 'system'. A system is a
network of interrelated points. In grammar, for

example, we talk about the 'tense system', which interrelates present, past, future and other notions. In pronunciation we talk about the 'vowel system', in which all the different vowels are shown in a relationship to each other. And it is the same with spelling. We have repeatedly seen in this book that there is a system underlying English spelling – a series of principles which have consistently guided the decision-making of writers over the centuries. The distinction between short and long vowel sounds is an example, with the associated doubling of consonant letters and the use of a final silent *e* (Chapters 6 and 7). Our perception of this system is often obscured by the many arbitrary decisions which have affected individual words, but it is present nonetheless. And the more we learn about the nature of the system, the more accessible English spelling becomes. Here are three examples.

First, the 'short word rule'. It doesn't take children very long before they notice a group of words in English that seem different from the others because of their size. These 'little words' are called, technically, 'grammatical' words, because their role is to show the grammatical structure of a sentence, relating the 'lexical' (or 'content-filled') words to each other. They occur frequently, as a result, and this is the reason that Old English scribes left them short: they were much easier to write. Orrm tried to make them conform to other words, and failed (Chapter 7).

It's possible to be more precise about what is

meant by 'little'. We can state a rule: lexical words in English are at least three letters long. It's a useful principle to be aware of, as it helps to explain several spellings that at first seem odd. Why do we spell a hostelry as an *inn* and not as an *in*? *In* was one of its spellings when it was first written down, along with *inn*; but eventually *inn* prevailed, allowing a clear contrast with the preposition *in*. Doubling the consonant was an easy way to make the word conform to the three-letter rule. We see it operating again with *Ann*, which might otherwise have been *An*, as well as *add*, *egg*, *ebb*, *odd*, *err*, *ill* and several more.

The letter *e* turns out to be a useful word-building element, as it helps short lexical words conform to the three-letter rule. *Bye* and *by* were both originally used as spellings for the preposition; but gradually the two-letter *by* was distinguished from the three-letter *bye*. Short spellings for *eye* and *owe* were avoided by keeping the silent final *e*. Sometimes other letters are silent. Those who spell the musical terms *do* as *doh*, *so* as *soh* and so on are reflecting the same trend.

Are there any exceptions to the three-letter rule? *Ox* and (US English) *ax* look like two, but they are a side-effect of the letter *x*, which represents two sounds /ks/. Two-letter abbreviations have to be allowed for, such as *ad*, *pa* (for father), *ex* (former partner) and *UN*. So do exclamations, such as *oy*, *oh* and *oo*, and the greeting *hi*. But these are clearly marginal cases. The only common words which are exceptions are *do* and *go*. A few more two-letter content words have come into English from foreign languages, such as *bo* (tree), *qi*, *om* and *pi*, and there are a few technical terms, such as *en* and *em* for different lengths of dash in printing. These are highly valued by Scrabble players.

A second example of a system at work is to recognise the importance of the way a word is stressed – a point already noted in Chapter 7. Why do some verbs ending in *-er* double the *r* when adding an ending, and others do not? We find *proffer* > *proffering* and *proffered*, but *prefer* > *preferring* and *preferred*. There is no explanation unless we recognise that words of the first type stress the first syllable, whereas words of the second type stress the second. Other examples like *proffer* are *enter*, *number*, *offer*, *suffer* and hundreds more. Words like *prefer* constitute a much smaller number, such as *confer*, *refer*, *deter* and *inter*, as well as a few verbs with slightly different endings, such as *disbar* and *abhor*. The principle is recognised when we make up new verbs. When the Internet began to use *spider* as a verb, the associated coinages were *spidering* and *spidered*. But if someone were to use *cigar* as a verb, we can be sure the derived forms would be spelled *cigarring* and *cigarred*.

A third example of a system lies in the way words are constructed – the subject of morphology. Consider a word-building exercise such as *problem, problematic, unproblematic*. We can show the structure thus: *un/problem/atic*. The slash marks indicate boundaries between the different meaningful elements (or *morphemes*). Several apparent spelling illogicalities can be explained by knowing whether there was such a boundary in the source language and where exactly it fell. Why is *aberrant* spelled with one *b* and *abbreviate* with two? Because they reflect the structure of the source words in Latin: *ab* + *errant* and *ab* + *breviate*. And that is why there is a double consonant in *adduce* (*ad* + *duce*) and *command* (*com* + *mand*), but no doubling in *adage* (*ad* + *agium*) and *comestible* (*com* + *edere*). Many words have doubled consonant letters because of the way the Latin prefix was followed by an identical consonant, such as *illegal* (*il* + *legal*) and *immodest* (*im* + *modest*). That is why there is a double *m* at the beginning of *commemorate* (*com* + *memorare*) and a single *m* in the middle.

One of the best-known spelling problems is explained by this reasoning: *accommodate*. Why two *c*s and two *m*s? Its root is the Latin word *modus* (meaning 'measure' or 'manner'). *Com* ('together with') was then placed in front, giving the double *m*. *Ad* ('to') was placed in front of that, with the *d* changing to a *c* for ease of pronunciation, giving the double *c*. Thus we get *ac* + *com* + *modate*. There's nothing irregular about the consonants at all – once we recognise the way the word is structured and are aware of the underlying prefixes. And if we know about its three-part structure, we are more likely to remember the spelling.

There are hundreds of 'difficult' words where an awareness of the etymology can help us predict whether they will contain a double consonant or not. Why *irresistible*, with two *rs*? Because it comes from *ir* + *resistere*. Why *occurrence* with two *cs*? Because it is from *oc* (earlier *ob*) + *currere*. And why is there no double *c* in *recommend* and *necessary*? Because there was no duplication in the Latin: *re* + *commendare*, *ne* + *cedere*. I find it hard to resist the conclusion that, if children were introduced to some basic etymology, many of the 'famous' spelling errors would be avoided.

There is one systematic exception to note. If the Latin prefix ends in *s* and the root begins with *s*, and is followed by a vowel, there is doubling in the usual way: *assent* (*as* from *ad* + *sentire*), *dissent* (*dis* + *sentire*), *dissect* (*dis* + *secare*). But if that *s* is followed by a consonant, there is no doubling: *ascribe* (*as* from *ad* + *scribere*), *transpire* (*trans* + *spirare*). It's a rule we respect in modern coinages. When a verb 'to make discordant in sound' was coined in the 1920s, it was spelled *dissonate* (*dis* + *sonare*). *Spatulate* ('to mix with a spatula') arrived in the same decade. There are as yet no verbs *dispatulate* or *transpatulate*, but if they were to be coined, that is how they would be spelled.

This is the ultimate test of the validity of a spelling principle: we use it to predict the spellings of words as yet unborn. For the young child, of course, most words in the language are unborn – in the sense that they are waiting to be learned. But the same requirement to anticipate applies to adults too, for none of us knows more than a fraction of the words

in the English language. Average educated vocabu-
laries are between 50,000 and 100,000 words; but
there are well over a million words in English, and
new ones are being coined all the time. To spell these
new words we apply our sense of existing principles. When we encounter a new word and feel that
it 'looks right' or 'looks wrong' without being sure
why, we are acknowledging these principles. Clearly,
the more we can bring these principles to the surface
of our consciousness, the more confident spellers we
will become.

There can never be a simple solution to the problem
of English spelling. We are faced with an orthography which is the result of over a millennium of
unpredictable social and linguistic change, and it
displays all the consequences of that unpredictability. The underlying system is robust and regular, but
struggles to be visible through the layers of orthographic practice introduced over the centuries by
writers with different linguistic, cultural and political backgrounds. Spelling reformers have repeatedly
tried to solve the problem, but failed. Educationists
have done their best, using a variety of methods,
but the problem seems as intractable as ever. Complaints continue to be made about a perceived fall in
spelling standards.

I believe, as army generals sometimes say, that
the best way of defeating an enemy is to get to understand him. My aim in this book, accordingly, has been

to provide a basic level of understanding about why we have a problem. I am convinced that the reason people find English spelling difficult is because they have not understood 'how it works'. The explanations are linguistic in character, to do with word history, word structure and the way sounds and letters inter-relate. I think this kind of perspective, which for the most part has been lacking in pedagogical practice, is essential. Spelling is a linguistic problem, which can be alleviated only by using linguistic tools. We are still some way from devising a spelling syllabus for schools based on sound linguistic principles, but I hope my account provides enough evidence to moti-vate educators to move in what I believe is a fresh and positive direction.

We have reached the present day, in the singular story of English spelling. But one thing more needs to be said – the story is not over yet. In a hundred years' time, our orthography will not look the same as it does today. What will be the differences?

George Crabbe on learning

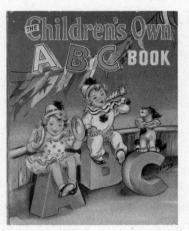

To learning's second seats we now proceed,
Where humming students gilded primers read;
Or books with letters large and pictures gay,
To make their reading but a kind of play –
'Reading made Easy', so the titles tell;
But they who read must first begin to spell:
There may be profit in these arts, but still
Learning is labour, call it what you will.

(George Crabbe, 'Letter 24: Schools', *The Borough*, 1810)

37

The future of English spelling

The Internet and globalisation are already affecting English spelling, and are likely to increase their influence. Simplified spelling is also a possibility.

It's never wise to predict the future, when it comes to language. Who would have anticipated, a thousand years ago, that Latin would one day cease to be a driving force in a child's education? Who, a mere twenty years ago, would have thought that the largest collection of written language ever would soon be found in a location called an 'Internet'? And who, just six years ago (I write in 2012), would have predicted that the next big thing on the Internet would be a short-messaging service in which people, in their millions, would report on what they are doing and on what's happening around them, and do so within a 140-character limitation in an unprecedented style (Twitter)? When language changes so rapidly and in such unexpected ways, we have to be extremely tentative in talking about its future, and the dimension of spelling is no exception.

We can be definite about one thing. Prophets

of doom have suggested that, because the Internet motivates so much spelling variation (Chapter 29), a standard English spelling system has no future. They are wrong. Exactly the opposite is the case. The Internet is the best guarantor we have of maintaining a standard spelling system, in all languages, because it relies for its efficacy on the accurate orthographic representation of words. Even the smallest spelling error in a domain name means we will be unable to access a website. And if a search term is wrongly spelled, our search may not work. The search engines, of course, do their best to anticipate the commonest typographic errors. If we type *busines* into Google, for example, we will be asked 'Did you mean *business?*' But Google throws in the towel if the deviant spelling goes beyond a certain point; and if the wrongly spelled word happens to coincide with an already existing word in the language (such as *busyness*), there will be no correction suggested at all.

This is the spell-checker problem I illustrated in my opening chapter. One of the consequences of the way the English spelling system has developed is that a large number of words differ by only a single letter. Indeed, word games have been based on this principle, such as Lewis Carroll's doublets. 'Drive PIG into STY' is one of his instructions. The player has to morph the first word into the second in the smallest number of moves, changing only one letter at a time. This is a five-move solution:

PIG > WIG > WAG > WAY > SAY > STY

It's easy to see why, if a single letter shift can cause such changes, the current spell checkers and search engines are soon out of their depth.

They will improve. A linguistically sophisticated generation of search tools will one day evolve, taking grammar, semantics and discourse structure into account. Grammar? The words will be tagged as nouns, verbs and so on, based on their position in the sentence and the way they are formed. A word which has an ending in *-ness* is probably going to be a noun (*goodness, happiness*, etc.). A word which has an ending in *-ly* is probably going to be an adverb (*happily, slowly*, etc.). Semantics and discourse? An analysis will be made of the meaning of a sentence, so that the right sense of a word will be identified, and this will be confirmed by taking into account the place of the sentence in the text as a whole. Seen as a single sentence, *The charge was successful* is ambiguous; but when we read the surrounding text it will be obvious whether it is about car batteries or military manoeuvres. As we saw in Chapter 28, the correct choice of a spelling may depend on getting the context right. No spell checker or search engine can currently do this kind of analysis. But one day …

Indeed, the day is not far off when the Internet, though totally spelling-dependent, will take the sting out of the task for the writer. As I mentioned in Chapter 1, speech-to-text technology already exists, and is improving year by year. Although there are many problems still to be faced, such as recognising broad accents, handling rapid speech and decoding rare words and unusual names, these will be much less serious within a generation or so. We will speak into our machines, and a reliable text will appear on screen before our eyes. This by no means eliminates the importance of spelling, of course. We still have to read what is written, and this requires the traditional decoding skills. We still have to allow for cases of deliberate non-standard usage, such as the examples given in Chapter 30. And there will always be cases where new words contain unpredictable spellings that need to be monitored before being added to the computer's dictionary. So the argument that the computer will make spelling irrelevant, and that future generations will no longer be able to spell, is false. In any case, these abilities are going to be required for the many everyday occasions when we need to use or react to written language and where we have no computer at our disposal – let alone those situations where our computer becomes useless because our battery has died or there has been a power cut.

The most interesting question is whether the Internet will allow us, in effect, to wind the clock back to an earlier and more regular period of English spelling, and introduce a modicum of spelling reform. In Chapter 29, I gave the example of non-standard *rubarb* emerging alongside *rhubarb*, and suggested that it was only a matter of time before *rubarb* became a recognised alternative, as has happened

to *judgment* and *judgement, realise* and *realize, encyclo-
paedia* and *encyclopedia, minuscule* and *miniscule,* and
many more word pairs. *Rubarb* is by no means alone.
Accommodate, occurrence and other words which have
caused special difficulty in the past may be simplified by writers who have internalised the basic principles of English spelling and who are following their
phonetic instincts to eliminate the grosser irregularities. It will take a lot of time for this to happen.
The power of received orthographic practice, and a
respect for tradition, makes it impossible for spelling
reform of this kind to take place overnight, or even
over-decade. But over-century, yes.

Another unpredictable outcome arises from the
emergence of English as a global language. One of
the penalties of success, when a language achieves
an international presence, is that any notion of own-
ership is lost. When English came to be adopted by
the USA, as we saw in Chapter 26, a new orthography arrived, expressing the identity of the new
nation. The British didn't like it at the time – indeed,
some still object to it – but there was not the slightest thing they could do about it. And the same sort
of development has taken place in several other parts
of the world where political independence has led to
new dialects, new accents, and – to an extent – new
spellings or combinations of spellings. Canadian
English, for example, is distinctive for the way it
combines British and American spelling. In Toronto,
'Sammy's Service Centre' (a British spelling)

advertises a 'Winter Tire Sale' (an American spelling). And when we read the writing of Caribbean poets such as Linton Kwesi Johnson, we see the way in which a new local identity fosters a fresh set of orthographic conventions. Here are the opening lines of his 'Mekkin Histri':

> *now tell mi someting*
> *mistah govahment*
> *tell mi someting*
> *how lang yu really feel*

Spelling variations of this kind can be found in all parts of the English-speaking world nowadays.

It is even more important, therefore, to adopt a linguistic – and specifically a sociolinguistic – frame of reference for the teaching of spelling. Learners need to be made aware of the regularities of the spelling system, of course, but they also need to be kept fully informed about the variation that is already there, why it is there, and where it is increasing. This means keeping up-to-date with the changes that are taking place as a result of the Internet and globalisation. A standard spelling system will continue to be important, but the range of alternatives that are accepted as standard will change. The more we understand the basis of spelling, how English has evolved its system, and where its strengths and weaknesses lie, the more we will be able to meet this future with confidence, as learners and teachers.

A linguistic perspective is especially important

when working with young people. Anyone born after 1991 (when the World Wide Web arrived) inhabits a world where the screen is central and traditional paper text is marginal. These 'natives' of the Internet have to learn to cope with an online orthographic diversity that is much greater than anything older people ever experienced on the printed page. Faced with a bewildering array of orthographic choices, they have to develop the confidence to make the right decisions for the written tasks they need to complete. The role of the teacher of spelling will be as important as it ever was, therefore, but the nature of the task will change. It will no longer be just a question of teaching learners to spell a word correctly but of showing them how to choose the appropriate spelling to suit the demands of the situation.

They will also need to be taught about social attitudes. Learners have to appreciate that they are living in a world which has both conservative and radical views about spelling, and that attitudes and expectations are deeply held. As I said in my Introduction, there are employers who will reject a job application simply because of the way it is spelled or because it uses an abbreviation felt to be inappropriate (such as *I hope I get the job :)* – a real example). These people exist in the same world as those who celebrate spelling idiosyncrasies and use them because of the effects they convey. The task facing the learner is thus to make an informed and confident choice. And the task facing the teacher is to understand and explain what is happening, so that the right advice can be given and the right choices made. A period of rapid transition, such as we are living through at the moment, inevitably makes both tasks more challenging.

Clearly, we need to develop new techniques of spelling management, and I make some suggestions in the appendices below. Doing nothing – that is, staying with traditional teaching models – is not an option. The Internet and globalisation are not going to go away. English will continue to change, as it always has, but more rapidly than it has for some time because of the way the Internet hastens the spread of innovation. Once, a new usage would have taken decades before it became noticed by the whole of the English-speaking community. Today, a linguistic novelty can be around the world in a matter of seconds. Spelling is not free from these processes of change. On the contrary: because it is always in front of our eyes, in every word and sentence that we write, we are likely to encounter orthographic novelty more often than innovations in vocabulary, grammar or punctuation.

Nor is staying with traditional attitudes towards spelling an option. We – everyone, not just teachers – need to change the way we think about it. We have to stop viewing it in solely negative terms – as a daunting barrier, as a hostile mountain, as an apparently perpetual process of rote learning – and start thinking of it as a voyage of exploration. The story of the English writing system is so intriguing, and the histories behind individual words so fascinating, that anyone who dares to treat spelling as an adventure will find the journey rewarding. It is a skill whose acquisition requires serious application, of course, but that does not need to be at the expense of enjoyment. Approached in the right way, spelling can be fun.

A teaching appendix

I *Avoiding isolation*

*Progress in learning to spell comes when words are taught
in realistic contexts, in sets of related items. The most useful
corrections of wrong spellings require an analysis which
diagnoses the cause of the errors.*

If we view English spelling as being, in essence, a system
of principles – albeit with many exceptions – a number
of teaching strategies immediately follow. And the most
important of all is this: words should never be taught out
of context.

Traditionally, words like *necessary, occurrence* and the
others are taught in isolation. The child is supposed
to learn them off by heart, and tries to do so, one at a
time. I recall being given 'ten difficult spellings a night'
in primary school. But because there are so many of
them, and without any way of seeing a pattern, the load
on the memory is often too great to be coped with – the
result being that many adults, even those who in other
respects are quite good at spelling, constantly need to
look these words up in a dictionary. Yet there is a principle
here, waiting to be noticed. *Necessary* is exactly like *recommend*, in its underlying structure, as we saw in Chapter

35. *Occurrence* is exactly like *accommodate*. There is system beneath the apparent irregularity.

With serious application, we can all learn lists of words. Every reader of this book has done so. But our residual uncertainties are evidence that the approach wasn't always successful; and many people found it hard to make progress, and today call themselves 'bad spellers'. The extent of the problem was hidden until recently by the lack of opportunity to display one's writing in public and the availability of copy-editors and proofreaders to correct spelling errors before they appeared in print. All this has changed, because of the Internet. As I pointed out in Chapter 29, people can now write in the public domain as much as they want, in blogs, chats, social networking posts, texts and tweets, and there is no cadre of editors correcting their spelling. Spelling checkers don't solve all the problems, as noted in my opening chapter; and they are in any case rarely used on the more interactive sites. As a result, we see non-standard spellings everywhere. Some commentators see this as a decline in standards. I don't. The problem has always been there. It is simply that now it is visible to everyone.

Lists go against all the basic principles of language acquisition. Nobody learns to speak through lists, and nobody should learn to write that way either. When a child learns to say a word, it simultaneously learns its pronunciation, meaning, grammar and role in the discourse. 'That's an elephant,' says a mother, pointing to a picture. 'Look at its big long trunk ...' Spoken words are always learned in association with other words and are embedded in sentences. It needs to be the same when children learn to read and write. What is a child to make of a list like this – a typical night's homework for a nine-year-old from many years ago?

handkerchief
necessary
foreign
mortgage
scissors
embarrass
Wednesday
separate
miniature
business
efficient

The list juxtaposes different types of spelling problem, words of different frequencies, and words of different levels of semantic difficulty – *handkerchief* and *scissors*, on the one hand; *miniature* and *mortgage* on the other. But more important, the likelihood that the child might encounter these words being used naturally in the same discourse is remote. It is an exercise totally removed from linguistic reality.

Such exercises are at their worst when they include the famous 'confusables', such as *principal* and *principle* or *stationary* and *stationery*. Placing such items in a list is of no use at all, as their pronunciation is identical. Rather, we have to see how the words are used, and associate the right spelling with the appropriate semantic and grammatical contexts. For example, an awareness of the concrete meaning of *principal* can be built up through exposure to such collocations as *principal boy, principal girl, principal trumpet* and *school principal*. An awareness of the abstract meaning of *principle* can be built up through such collocations as *in principle, on principle, first principles* and *basic principles*. The meaning of *principal* motivates its use largely in singular contexts; the meaning of *principle* motivates its use in plural contexts. The words should always be seen in sentences, never in isolation.

The same strategy is needed with *stationary* and *stationery*. A grammatical reminder here would be the distinction between noun (*buying some stationery*) and adjective (*the traffic was stationary*). A semantic reminder would be to connect *stationery* to *envelope*, for example, with memory reinforcement coming from the repeated *e*s; or *stationary* to *halt*, with the repeated *a*s. What must be avoided at all costs is to teach both words at the same time in 'clever' contexts, such as *The stationary van was carrying stationery* or *The principal had principles*. That is not how vocabulary is naturally learned, and it is not a natural way of learning to spell either.

Juxtapositions of this kind are unnatural in a further respect. They give the impression that the two words are equally likely. In fact, there are always differences of frequency. If we search for the above items in the Wiktionary frequency lists, which use a corpus of over 1.7 billion words, we find that *stationary* is over three times more frequent than *stationery*. If we search in Google, we find that *principal* is ten times more likely to be encountered than *principle*. These are important guidelines for teaching. Quite clearly, the spelling of *stationary* and *principal* should be established before their alternates, and similarly with all other word pairs which sound the same. If word frequency is taken into account, there should never be any confusion between a high-occurring item such as *carrot* and a low-occurring one such as *caret*, for the former will be well established before the latter is ever encountered; and similarly for *cash* and *cache*, *born* and *borne*, *council* and *counsel*, *ark* and *arc*, and many more.

The principle of 'word-families' – here meaning groups

of words sharing the same root – also aids learning, as the spellings reinforce each other. As long as the words share a similar likelihood of encounter, for a child of a particular age, then it must help to see them used together – *principal* and *principally*, for example, or *stationer* and *stationery*. In many cases, several words are involved, as with *necessary, necessity, necessarily, necessitate, unnecessary* ... and *separate, separation, separated, separable, unseparable* ... The approach is particularly useful with groups like *sign, signs, signing, signal, signalling* ..., where the sounded *g* of *signal* can be a mnemonic for the silent *g* of the other words. The family approach can be extended to parts of words, such as the *to* of *today, tonight, tomorrow, together* ... The principle is just as relevant for adult learning too, both in remedial settings and in those where English is being taught as a foreign language.

Avoiding isolation is also crucial when it comes to marking written work and identifying spelling mistakes. There is limited value in the routine practice of underlining an error, crossing out or inserting a letter, or writing in the correct form, as in these examples:

> *He ommitted the date at the top of the page.* Teacher correction: the second *m* crossed through.
> *It was a catastrophy.* Teacher correction: the *y* crossed out and an *e* written above.
> *The result was innaccurate.* Teacher correction: the second *n* crossed out.
> *I wrote a pome about it.* Teacher correction: *poem* written above the word.
> *I reconised the place.* Teacher correction: *g* inserted.
> *I went to the libry.* Teacher correction: *ar* inserted.
> *The cows were in the feild.* Teacher correction: *field* written above the word.

We ate ice creams. Teacher correction: hyphen inserted
  between *ice* and *creams*.

These corrections identify the errors but they do not
explain them. To adopt a medical analogy, this approach
identifies symptoms, but fails to make a diagnosis – and
one needs a diagnosis before one can proceed to a cure.

There are several different kinds of error in these
examples. Why would children ever go to the trouble of
adding an extra *m* in *omit*, when there is not even a short
vowel sound to suggest it? Probably because they have a
visual memory of another word where there are two *ms*
and the same stress pattern: *commit*. Why add an extra *n*
to make *innaccurate*? Probably because of the influence of
words like *inner* and *innocent*. Why *catastrophy*? Because
they are remembering words which end in *-y*, especially
(in this case) *trophy*. In such cases, we see the operation
of analogy (Chapter 17) – the same process of reasoning
which influenced scribes centuries ago. Progress here will
depend on recognising the sources of graphic interference
and devising ways of distinguishing them.

Cases like *pome*, *reconized* and *libry* are very different.
Here the error comes from writing the word as it is pronounced in colloquial speech. Many wrong spellings have
this source, such as *litrature*, *bankrupcy* and *govemment*.
Progress here will depend on recognising the stylistic
character of the problem – the contrast between formal
and informal pronunciation – and the various kinds of
phonetic effect involved. It is possible to draw attention
to the problem in *library* by saying the word slowly, so that
one hears the unstressed medial syllable. But this solution is not possible for *government*, where the medial consonant is never pronounced, even in formal speech. Here,

a word-family approach is needed – relating *government* to *govern*, *governor* and so on.

Feild is different again. Here the writer has lost track of the norms and exceptions which affect this sequence of letters, and we would expect to find other words in this person's writing displaying similar errors, such as *thier* and *freind*. No diagnosis of *feild* can succeed if that word is viewed in isolation. The writer's general grasp of the *ie / ei* distinction needs to be explored (Chapter 26).

For many writers, *ice cream* would not be an error at all, as usages with and without a hyphen are both current, and the writer needs to be made aware of this. The important thing here is consistency. If the writer chooses a hyphen-ated form, this should be repeated each time the form is used in a single piece of writing. It would thus be impor-tant for the teacher to check with colleagues that the same correction is being made by them too, in order to ensure a consistency of approach across the curriculum; and the same concern should surface in relation to any other words where present-day usage allows alternatives, such as *judg-ment* and *judgement* (Chapter 28). All of this should be part of a school's language policy. There is nothing more con-fusing than to have one's spelling errors corrected in dif-ferent ways by different teachers – unless, of course, it is not to have one's errors corrected at all!

II *Towards a linguistics of spelling*

Spelling is a unique skill; it is the bridge which interrelates reading and writing. Views about how to teach it have varied greatly, and an important part of getting to grips with it is to understand what the different approaches are and why they have changed. A linguistic perspective is essential.

Literacy involves three skills, not two: reading, writing – and spelling. Traditionally, just the first two skills were recognised – and this emphasis is still with us. The typical dictionary definition (as in the *Oxford English Dictionary*) states that literacy is the 'ability to read and write'. No mention of spelling.

Spelling needs to be given separate acknowledgement, as it is a unique skill. It is different from reading. In reading, someone else has done all the work, writing the words down. It is possible to read by attending selectively to the cues in a text, recognising a few letters and guessing the rest. It isn't possible to spell in this way: spellers have to identify *all* the letters. Also, more things can go wrong while spelling. As pointed out in earlier chapters, there are far more spellings for a sound than there are pronunciations for a letter. There is really only one way to say the letter sequence *deep*, but there are several ways of writing the sound sequence /di:p/, such as *deep, depe* and *deap*.

Spelling is also different from writing. We see this clearly in spelling bees and other competitions. It is not just a matter of knowing the names of the letters and speaking them aloud; the speller must also hold the letter sequence of the whole word in mind while naming the letters in the correct order. This is where competitors often make an error. They know the spelling all right, but something goes wrong in the speaking of it, and the right letters come out in the wrong order. We might call this the 'Pooh effect', after A. A. Milne's character, who complained: 'My spelling is Wobbly. It's good spelling but it Wobbles, and the letters get in the wrong places' (*Winnie-the-Pooh*, Chapter 6).

Spelling also lacks the automaticity we associate with handwriting or typing. Whether we are spelling the words correctly or not, our hand/fingers can often perform the task without the brain paying any special attention. The clearest case is when we write our signature. We do it in a single action, and do not think out the name 'letter by letter'. This 'memory in the hand' can be seen at work in other situations. I once asked a concert pianist how he remembered all the pieces he played, and he replied 'the memory is in the fingers'. This is analogous to the letter sequences which are so frequent and familiar that our writing hand or fingers produce them automatically, often – in such cases as *and* and *the*, or the endings *-tion* and *-ing* – running the letters together in the process and ignoring such details as crossing a *t* or putting a dot over an *i*.

Spelling is neither reading nor writing. It is a separate skill, and it needs individual attention. A concern to achieve 'true orthography' in writing developed during the 16th century, but the general assumption was that, once a child had learned to read, the ability to spell would automatically follow. In 1582, Richard Mulcaster commented in his *Elementarie* (p. 22): 'the direction of his hand, whereby he learns to write, shall be answerable to his reading'. The view lasted a long time. In 1750, Lord Chesterfield remarked, in one of his letters to his son (19 November), 'Reading with care will secure everybody from false spelling.'

But attitudes were changing during the 18th century, as notions of correctness evolved and dictionaries became authorities (Chapter 25). Spelling became a primary criterion of educatedness, too important to be left to chance: it had to be 'taught', not 'caught'. As a result, the formal teaching of spelling through letter-naming, word tables, spelling rules and word-lists of increasing complexity became routine. We enter a classroom era when rule jingles (Chapter 24) were recited in unison, errors were corrected by repeated copying ('Write out 100 times ...'), and spellings were given as homework. Memory drills and spelling bees (a term first recorded in 1876) became regular experiences.

But by the end of the 19th century, teachers were becoming increasingly dissatisfied with this approach – as were parents. They were trying to teach rules that clearly did not work (Chapter 24). Words were being spelled in isolation, regardless of their meaning and relevance. The spelling lists were teaching children words they did not want to use in their writing, and were omitting words which they did want to use. The expected improvements were not taking place. Huge amounts of time were being devoted to teaching spelling which, some educators believed, could more usefully be devoted to other things. In 1897 an American physician-turned-educator, Joseph Mayer Rice, published a study called *The Futility of the Spelling Grind*. It was one of several over the next few decades showing there was no clear relationship between the amount of time devoted to learning about spelling, using the traditional methods, and the actual achievement of spellers. There was no appreciable difference in spelling accuracy among students who had been taught by formal instruction and those who had not.

During the 20th century, accordingly, the pendulum swung back towards the importance of reading. The idea resurfaced that increasing the quantity of one's reading would, more than anything else, be the simplest and best way to improve spelling. At the same time, a new emphasis emerged in relation to writing: creative content should be the priority, and should not be held back by an excessive concern to 'get the spelling right'. Some interpreted this new direction to mean that 'spelling was unimportant'. Cases were reported of spelling errors remaining uncorrected in schoolwork. And as complaints grew (for example, among employers) about poor standards of spelling, a return to traditional methods was advocated. The issue of spelling became controversial, and the controversy is still with us.

In my view, it is an unnecessary controversy, because the truth lies somewhere between the two extremes. Rules and lists can be helpful if they are the *right* rules and lists. The problem with the 19th-century methods was that they weren't. The lists contained large numbers of irrelevant words, and the rules were badly expressed or simply wrong. A word-list containing the words that a child actually wants to write can be very helpful, and if rules are replaced by explanations based on linguistic principles, as I argue in this book, formal teaching can be illuminating. At the same time, there is clearly huge value in getting children to read as much as possible – and I include here not only traditional books and magazines, but text messages, web pages, blogs, social interaction sites and other online sources. Spelling is a matter of internalising letter sequences in words, and the more opportunities they have to see these sequences the better. All the evidence suggests that the more children see spellings, whether regular or irregular, in their reading, the more readily they will start to use them in their writing.

We now know far more about what goes on when people write than we did a century ago. A major part of the process is drafting – something which takes place with all writing intended for public view (which is where spelling is going to be chiefly noticed). This book went through several drafts before it achieved its final form; and in its early drafts I left my typing errors uncorrected. The important thing was to get the ideas down and roughly expressed. A long process of polishing followed. Children need to learn how to do this, as part of the business of learning to write. Teachers nowadays routinely point out the value of note-making, story diagrams, drafting, re-reading and other strategies, and a focus on correct spelling is an important part of the process – but this should be left to a late stage, just before the text is allowed out into the public domain. It should not interfere with the creative processes involved in the earlier stages.

Word-lists can form a part of this process, but – as already mentioned – they have to be the right words. If you have to write a story about a visit to a zoo, what 'zoo-ey' words will you use to describe the setting or to add atmosphere? If you can think them up for yourself, all well and good – but what if you cannot? This is where a list of words relevant to the task can be extremely helpful, either provided by the teacher, or by a reading book, or by a lexical reference work of some kind.

When I am stuck for a word, I often turn to a thesaurus to stimulate my thinking. A thesaurus is a type of word-list. It doesn't replace my creativity – it offers me choices to enhance my creativity. The words I see are relevant to what I want to write because I have chosen to look in the right place for them – in this example, the 'zoo' section of the thesaurus.

A thesaurus is different from a dictionary. I use a dictionary because I know a word and want to look up its meaning. I use a thesaurus for the opposite reason: I know an area of meaning and I want to look up some words to talk about it. A good thesaurus contains all the information I need to establish word-families (Appendix I), and it presents these words in their standard spellings. If I am unsure how to spell a word, I will get this information from my thesaurus as easily as from my dictionary – sometimes more easily, in fact. If I do not know that *phantom* begins with *ph*, I will have a real problem finding it in a dictionary, but I will find it easily in the section on supernatural beings in a thesaurus.

Thus I see it as critical to provide children with simple thesauruses as they learn to write, in which the word-families are chosen to reflect their developmental level, their interests and their reading. These days, they need to reflect relevant Internet content too. And, just as we can add items of personal interest to the predictive list in our mobile phones, so there should be an opportunity for children to personalise their thesauruses, so that they contain words of private relevance to them – such as family names, brand-names, and place names. This can easily be done online, where there are unprecedented opportunities for self-correction and interaction, but it can be done on paper too.

Spelling is a bridge between reading and writing. If a child is being taught to read using a phonic method, the approach will instil a sense of the core regularity within the English spelling system. If a whole-word method is being used, it will instil a sense of the serial probability of letter sequences – that *q* is likely to be followed by *u*, that *-tion* is often used at the end of a word, that *v* at the end of a word is usually followed by *e* and so on. Phonic approaches enable us to evaluate whether a word 'sounds right' when they are reading. Visual approaches enable us to say whether a word 'looks right' when they are writing.

With a system like English, both approaches are needed; neither can give us the whole orthographic picture. How do you write a word like *window*, asks a child? 'Find the letters by sounding it out' is a familiar answer, but the result on the page needs to be followed by 'Does it look right?' Children develop an ability to tell the difference between a correct and incorrect spelling very early, especially when the word is part of their everyday visual experience. And it's a valuable strategy for adults too, whether native speakers or foreign learners.

Further reading

Beard, Roger (1993) *Teaching Literacy: Balancing Perspectives*. London: Hodder & Stoughton.

Carney, Edward (1994) *A Survey of English Spelling*. London & New York: Routledge.

—— (1997) *English Spelling*. London & New York: Routledge.

Cook, Vivian (2004) *Accomodating Brocolli in the Cemetary: Or Why Can't Anybody Spell?* London: Profile Books.

Hogg, Richard M. (ed.) (1992–9) *The Cambridge History of the English Language*, Vols 1–3. Cambridge: Cambridge University Press.

Mountford, John (1998) *An Insight into English Spelling*. London: Hodder & Stoughton.

Scragg, D. G. (1974) *A History of English Spelling*. Manchester: Manchester University Press; New York: Barnes & Noble Books.

Upward, Christopher and George Davidson (2011) *The History of English Spelling*. Chichester & Malden: Wiley-Blackwell.

Wolman, David (2008) *Righting the Mother-Tongue: From Olde English to Email, the Tangled Story of English Spelling*. New York: HarperCollins.

Yule, Valerie (2005) *The Book of Spells and Misspells*. Lewes: The Book Guild.

Illustration Credits

While every effort has been made to contact copyright-holders of illustrations,
the author and publishers would be grateful for information about any
illustrations where they have been unable to trace them, and would be glad to
make amendments in further editions.

Index of Words

General Index

General American 16–19
Geneva Bible 155, 184
German loanwords 244
Gershwin, George and Ira 183
ghost words 258
gh spellings 83–5, 138–42,
    169–73
Gill, Alexander 154
globalisation 274–5, 277
Gnu Song 166
Google searches 211, 221, 271,
    282
Government Printing Office
    205, 207
grammar 50, 114, 176, 180,
    185, 261–2, 272, 281–3
grammatical words 56, 262
graphic design 214
Great Vowel Shift 129–35
Greek 26–31, 100
    loans 73, 145, 158, 161, 163,
    167, 247
Greenbaum, Sidney 210
greengrocer's apostrophe 240
Guardian, The 207
gui spellings 124

h
    class differences 65
    doubling 63–4
    in *ghost* etc 138–41
    problems 32, 60, 82–3, 244
hair salons 225
Hamlet 140
handwriting 104–9
Hare, Archbishop 200
Hart, Horace 101, 206–7
Hart, John 78, 154
Hart's Rules 207
heavy/light spelling 54–8
heavy/light words 133–4
Henry, O 241
History of English Spelling, A 1
Hoccleve, Thomas 150–51

Holmes, Oliver Wendell 209
Holofernes 155–6
homographs 117–19
homophones 114–19
Horrid Henry 203
house names 226
house style 139, 206–8, 219,
    257
hyphenation 208, 213–14, 259,
    285

i
    alternating with *y* 105–6,
        180–81, 233, 239
    before *e* 177–85, 285
    distinct from *j* 93–4, 103,
        190
    with dot 105
I Before E (Except After C) 179
identity 212–13, 223–34,
    245–7, 274–5
incaps 217
indexers 213
inflections 43, 106, 113, 180
ink-horn words 69–70, 145
intercaps 217
interjections 249–52, 263
Internet 216–21, 259–60, 264,
    270, 275, 277, 280, 289, 291
Irish writing 24, 79
irregularity 124, 138–9, 150, 173
isolation, avoiding 279–85, 288
Italian loanwords 106–7, 141

j
    distinct from *i* 93–4, 105,
        190
    doubling 63
    final 243
Jefferson, Thomas 178
Jerome, St 13
Johnson, Dr 75, 87, 101, 141,
    162, 177, 188–95, 197, 201,
    206

DATE			